Anatomy of Miracles

Subagh Singh Khalsa

ANATOMY

Practical Teachings for Developing

OF

Your Capacity to Heal

MIRACLES

Tuttle Publishing

BOSTON · RUTLAND, VERMONT · TOKYO

First published in 1999 by Tuttle Publishing, an imprint of Periplus Editions (HK) Ltd., with editorial offices at 153 Milk Street, Boston, Massachusetts, 02109.

LIBRARY OF CONGRESS CATALOGING-PUBLICATION DATA

Khalsa. Subagh Singh,
    Anatomy of miracles : practical teachings for developing your capacity to heal / Subagh Singh Khalsa.—1st ed.
        p.   cm.
    ISBN 1–885203–73–X (hc)
    1. Spiritual healing.   I. Title
    BL65.M4K43   1999
    291.3'1–dc21   99–17806

Distributed by

USA
Tuttle Publishing
Distribution Center
Airport Industrial Park
364 Innovation Drive
North Clarendon, VT 05759-9436
Tel: (802) 773-8930
Tel: (800) 526-2778

JAPAN
Tuttle Shokai Ltd
1-21-13, Seki
Tama-ku, Kawasaki-shi
Kanagawa-ken 214-0022, Japan
Tel: (044) 833-0225
Fax: (044) 822-0413

CANADA
Raincoast Books
8680 Cambie Street
Vancouver, British Columbia
V6P 6M9
Tel: (604) 323-7100
Fax: (604) 323-2600

SOUTHEAST ASIA
Berkeley Books Pte Ltd
5 Little Road #08-01
Singapore 536983
Tel: (65) 280-1330
Fax: (65) 280-6290

First edition
05 04 03 02 01 00 99   10 9 8 7 6 5 4 3 2 1

Book design by Christopher Kuntze
Printed in the United States of America

With intense gratitude
I dedicate this book to Yogi Bhajan,
my spiritual teacher. In his humility and in
the vastness of his vision, this great Master has
always asked of his students only one thing:
that each of us become ten times
greater than he.

CONTENTS

PRACTICE EXERCISES

INTRODUCTION

L EARNING Sat Nam Rasayan is exactly like learning to
control a muscle. I remember, as a teenager, learning to
walk again after a serious accident that almost caused
me to lose my left leg. For many weeks I couldn't use my leg
at all. Only slowly did I develop trust in my leg muscles, and
regain my coordination, and my confidence that I could walk
and run and use the muscles skillfully. At first I hesitated to
use my leg—I needed to build up my muscles slowly, gradually gaining confidence. The process I went through is not unlike the sensitive process of Sat Nam Rasayan. At first you
may not even recognize that you have these healing muscles.
You may have no faith in your capacity to help another to
heal. It may take time to trust yourself to use these muscles
and learn to use them easily. Gradually, as you practice, you
will gain in skill, just as I slowly became more able to walk.
Gradually you will heal without thinking, just as I became
able to walk without considering every step. At some point
you will realize that you can trust the muscles to do as you
wish and that you can count on them. Eventually you will use
the healing capacity as easily as you use any other healthy part
of yourself. As you work through this book you will learn
that Sat Nam Rasayan is much more than technique, more,

that is, than a collection of particular skills applied in particular situations. Rather, the practice of Sat Nam Rasayan is based on learning how to bring oneself into a state of heightened awareness and neutrality while holding an intention to heal. This, you will soon see, can be enormously effective.

Using the simple process described in this book you will learn to help yourself and others be rid of the inner tendencies that can cause disease. You will do this by entering into and working in particular states of consciousness, states we call the "sensitive space" and, at a more advanced level of practice, the "Sacred Space." The exercises in this book will be your guide as you bring yourself into these very particular spiritual states in which healing happens due to your presence. I will share with you a rather systematic and easily traveled path to arrive at these states of consciousness so that you can help yourself and others to heal. I will not try to describe to you what you might expect to find in these "spaces"—I shall leave that daunting task to the poets. But I will tell you how to get there, and this I know will serve you well.

A few words here about terms might help to avoid confusion. The "sensitive space" is a method. It is the way that you will exercise your conscious mind as you approach Sat Nam Rasayan. A synonymous expression is "the sensitive process," and I will use these two terms interchangeably. The "Sacred Space" of Sat Nam Rasayan (which I will always capitalize) is a very particular transcendent state beyond everyday consciousness. One way to arrive at that state—the way we will be using here—is through the sensitive process.

These spiritual spaces, or states, have no doubt been discovered and rediscovered throughout the ages by any number of masters and mystics, but it was in the sixteenth century in the person of Guru Ram Das, the great Indian saint and the fourth Guru of the Sikh faith, that our present lineage was established. Guru Ram Das was the architect of the Golden Temple, the holiest shrine of the Sikhs. He began the building of this marvelous structure in the center of a large tank of water noted for its miraculous healing powers. Today, thousands of worshipers go there every day to drink from and bathe in these holy waters, and to meditate and be healed.

Guru Ram Das became the exemplar who recognized, embodied, and passed on the specific state of consciousness that we today call the Sacred Space of Sat Nam Rasayan. Guru Ram Das is known for his supreme humility and his teaching that one cannot be fulfilled by religious ritual or even by solitary meditation, but only by actively participating in the relief of the sorrows and suffering of others. His name, Ram Das, means "servant of God," and he taught that one could rid oneself of the primal malady of ego only by serving the God in others. It was in this spirit that he established the lineage of Sat Nam Rasayan that has sustained the Sacred Space for over four hundred years.

One of the conditions of the Sat Nam Rasayan lineage is that, unlike most other spiritual disciplines, it was not established primarily to serve the personal needs of its practitioners. In fact, the only purpose of Sat Nam Rasayan is healing —a condition that has helped to maintain its purity. Yet the sensitive process and the Sacred Space are powerful meditative states that benefit *anyone* who enters them, and anyone who serves the healing needs of another will certainly be blessed for the effort. One can also use Sat Nam Rasayan for self-healing. Moreover, the lessons of Sat Nam Rasayan— lessons about the true meanings of awareness, love, and

3

compassion—and the transcendent experience gained through its practice, will inform every aspect of a committed practitioner's life. Those who follow the path of Sat Nam Rasayan will find it very liberating indeed.

Spirituality is so simple; not necessarily easy, mind you, but very, very simple. Growing up as a Roman Catholic, I was taught from the very beginning that our reason for being is to "know, love, and serve God," the All-in-All, what some call the Absolute, or the Universal Mind, or the Void, or any of a thousand other names (each of which is utterly unable to convey even an iota of the meaning that it strives to indicate). But how does one "know God"?

Consider that you are, essentially, a point of consciousness, without dimension. Having taken life in a material form you have from the very beginning of this life developed a complex idea of your "self" as body, mind, emotions, feelings, roles played, relationships, and so on. You have developed an overpowering urge to protect this self and will tend to do so at almost any cost. Your beliefs tell you that you need certain things and had better avoid others. Desires and fears rule your life, often without your being very conscious of them. But in the midst of this structure you call "I" remains the true self; that original single point of consciousness. This point, this very center, this original self, is God in you, the ultimate reality.

Spiritual practice is returning to an awareness of yourself as that point—understanding the simple truth that you and God are one. Meditation is how we tread the spiritual path. In meditation we allow our erroneous beliefs about who we are to drop away, and we bring our attention ever closer to our original self. Instead of struggling to get all the details of our life in order as a way of finding happiness, we focus in-

4

stead on learning to experience things as they are, burdened by neither fear nor desire. As we do this we draw closer to the central point of consciousness. But no one has ever formulated a reliable method for taking the last step into actual knowledge of the Infinite. Many have taught how to approach the Infinite, to knock at its door as it were, but none have told us how to actually open that final door. That happens, not by our efforts, but by the final surrender of all effort and by what is called "grace." This is the moment of enlightenment, of seeing the light of which we are a part, of letting our light blend with the boundless light. Only then do we know God.

In Sat Nam Rasayan, the sensitive process is how we meditate, how we approach God's door. With this process we practice knowing the only thing we can ever really know: the experience of this moment. That practice keeps us right up against the door, pressed hard against it, as it were, insistently knocking, waiting for the moment of grace, when it is opened from the other side so we may know God.

And what does it mean to "love God"? This is not some great affection for all the good things of life or a deep desire to merge into the light. That would be too easy. To love God is to love what is, even if it is repugnant to our human tastes. If all is One then all that happens is also One, and to love the One is to love all that happens. How is this to be accomplished? How can we love the murdering terrorist, love the cancer, or love the starvation of a generation of orphans in a country ravaged by civil war? This becomes possible only when we recognize that love and affection are two vastly different things.

Love is the ability to allow what is, as it is, without resistance. Faced with the horror of a starving child, or of an abusive spouse, no one asks that we like that horror, but true spirituality does demand that we learn to allow within ourselves, without resistance, the experience we have when we witness it. If we become capable of allowing the pain we feel then we also become capable of allowing whoever or whatever has engendered that pain. This is the original source of compassion and love. Faced with a homeless alcoholic begging money from us, do we turn away from her, unable to handle our own fear and loathing? Or are we able to allow those feelings to arise and pass on through us without resistance—like smoke through a gossamer screen? When the latter is the case, when we have learned to be present with our own experience, then we can also be present with the beggar, and practice compassion for her suffering. Similarly we can forgive the cruel and love the disease.

This "allowing" is the central teaching of Sat Nam Rasayan. Allowing and the sensitive process are how we develop our presence. It is how we learn to love God and to heal.

Finally, how is it that one can "serve God"? Is there something that God needs that we can provide? To answer this, again understand that all is One, everything you might ever see or feel is a part of one indivisible whole. When we suffer, it is not our suffering; it is suffering in the world. When a child is starving it is not only one child who starves but it is a starvation that we all share in. Our enlightenment, our liberation, is not for us alone. They are for all beings. They are how we reduce suffering in the world. It is not just that we need to reduce our *own* suffering and find our *own* happiness; that is the path of ego. Rather, we are to serve God, and God is the All-in-All, so we serve God by making an effort to reduce suffering, wherever we may see it.

This service is also an integral part of Sat Nam Rasayan. Our practice is for healing, for reducing suffering in others and in ourselves, wherever it is found. Such service is what a liberated or enlightened person does—it is the expression of the spiritual in action.

There is no ceremony or special ritual associated with Sat Nam Rasayan, and it is not associated with any particular religion or spiritual path. The Sacred Space is entirely free of predetermined form or structure, and there is no set appearance to what you will be doing. Other than healing, there is no one thing that is expected to happen. The only requirement is that practitioners enter the Space, be able to hold themselves there without wavering, all the while maintaining the intention to heal.

The exercises I will guide you through in this book are part of the sensitive process. They are the path but not the destination. They are how you will initially learn to enter the Sacred Space, but they are not themselves that Space. Nor are they the only possible way to approach Sat Nam Rasayan. They are efficient, however, and a moderate amount of practice will yield gratifying results.

In gross anatomy lab at dental school I peeled back my cadaver's scalp, opened the cranium and removed the brain. The brain was cut in two and its parts examined during many hours of meticulous dissection. The same was done to the chest and the heart, the neck, the jaw, the abdomen. Day after day, week after week, I searched for the tiniest parts, experiencing a sense of triumph when I located and labeled some obscure nerve or vein, and a sense of failure when I mistook a small accumulation of fat for an endocrine gland. I was incompetent at first, and nervous, but bit by bit I gained confidence and competence, and at the end of the course I tried to believe that I knew the body.

I didn't of course, I only knew a little about its component parts and their juxtaposition to one another. How did all this stuff come together to create life? How did this cadaver at one time have consciousness and feeling and function? The miracle of the body completely eluded me, even as I mastered its anatomy. The body is both a miracle not fully understood by the human mind, and a collection of interrelated functions that, in fact, can be understood. We know more and more about how muscles contract and how the brain sends the signal to make them do so, yet life itself remains as mysterious and miraculous as ever.

But is the unexplained unexplainable? Does our incomplete understanding of the functioning of living organisms imply that they cannot ever be understood? What about the "miracle" of healing? Can we learn enough of the components of healing to understand the essence of it? Can we dissect healing, comprehend the meaning and juxtaposition of its parts, and somehow put it all together in a way that makes the miracle fully understandable—not a miracle at all but a learnable process?

My answer is a qualified "yes." Yes, you can dissect healing, practice the component parts, and eventually arrive at a subjective understanding of the process in full. That is what these exercises are for. There is only one small caveat: the understanding you will arrive at will not be an objective, intellectual understanding. You will know healing in a different, nonrational, way—in your soul, perhaps, or in your tissues, but not so completely in your head. At that point what you do as healer will not seem so miraculous to you. To you it will just be something you do, as easily as you walk down a street, needing only to hold to the intention of arriving at your destination.

In the end healing is as much a miracle as life itself, as

Introduction

much a miracle as walking. Our task here is to make it, like walking, an everyday miracle.

Since the days of Guru Ram Das, and until very recently, Sat Nam Rasayan was a hidden tradition, passed down through the generations in the old way, as were so many other esoteric traditions. A master of Sat Nam Rasayan would have one or two disciples and over a period of years would test and guide them. At some point a disciple might transcend all the limiting concepts in his or her mind and would directly experience the meaning of the teachings. When this happened the master would recognize the disciple's breakthrough and help the disciple to recognize his or her own achievement. Eventually the successful disciple would have disciples of his or her own, and so the tradition and lineage of Sat Nam Rasayan was perpetuated.

In 1969 Yogi Bhajan, master of Kundalini and White Tantric Yoga, and also at that time the only living person who knew the Sacred Space, came to the West from India and became the first person to teach Kundalini and White Tantric Yoga publicly. Previously only the most advanced students of yoga had access to these techniques, but Yogi Bhajan knew that it was time for the old system to change. He also recognized the great need in our time for healers and that it was no longer appropriate to maintain Sat Nam Rasayan as a hidden tradition. His approach to this situation was as radical as his open teaching of Kundalini and White Tantric Yoga had been. One last time he transmitted Sat Nam Rasayan in the old way. He taught it to one of his students, a man from Mexico who had also been trained in the native healing traditions of his country. This man, whose name is Guru Dev Singh, was then given the task of teaching Sat Nam Rasayan to others. But, in giving Guru Dev this assignment, Yogi Bhajan stipulated that

9

he could no longer teach in the traditional way. Guru Dev would have to create a systematic approach to the Sacred Space, a method that anyone could practice individually, in public classes, or in study groups. A state of consciousness that had been previously taught or induced between a master and a disciple was now to be taught in a contemporary workshop format. Guru Dev set about devising a method to teach Sat Nam Rasayan verbally and through practical exercises. Through his effort the lineage is now being passed on, not to a few disciples, but to thousands of students of the school of Sat Nam Rasayan that he has established. Guru Ram Das's consciousness remains present in the school and in anyone who is healing within this lineage.

Essentially, the system that Guru Dev Singh created is based on using the inherent sensitivity of the student to produce or arrive at an altered state of consciousness. The system is the "sensitive space" or the "sensitive process" and is the way that Sat Nam Rasayan is now being taught. Using the sensitive process is like learning the letters of the alphabet and sounding out words when you were learning to read. You needed to do that at first even though it was not what an expert reader would do. Sounding out words lets you get some sense of the meaning, but it was an inefficient process. Later, with practice, there came a time when you were reading effortlessly without having to think about the reading process at all. It is the same with our sensitive process. It will allow you to heal because it will give you the capacity to help another to relax deeply and let go of harmful patterns that can cause tension or disease. Later you will mature in your practice and enter the much more efficient Sacred Space. Compared to the Sacred Space, the sensitive process is slower, although it does facilitate healing. While the Sacred Space is a purely spiritual healing space, the sensitive space or process is physical. It will help you become highly aware of sensory experience, and stabilize your consciousness—you will learn how not to be distracted.

As you read further in this book, and do the practice exercises, you will acquire a better understanding of our two spaces. For now, simply understand that the sensitive space or process is the way you will be learning to heal. Later, if you keep up your practice and have proper guidance, you will experience the Sacred Space. The sensitive space, for all its wonderful benefits, is just the beginning. The Sacred Space, being in the realm of spirit, has no limit.

For this book to be of maximum benefit, you will need to spend time practicing the techniques it teaches. These are your basic tools, and their use should be mastered. The more practice the better. I also strongly recommend that you do a regular practice of Kundalini Yoga and Meditation as taught by Yogi Bhajan—nothing will prepare you so well to hold yourself stable in the healing space. In the Resources page at the end of the book, I give you a phone number to call for the name of a Kundalini Yoga teacher near you. An experienced teacher and a regular yoga class will be a great support to you on your way. Other spiritual practices can also help as you develop your meditative stability.

Another invaluable experience will be for you to take a Sat Nam Rasayan class or workshop. Guru Dev Singh, along with student-instructors under his direct supervision, teaches these workshops worldwide, and in them you will be guided to experience the Sacred Space. The Resources page also includes a phone number to call for information about these classes. Finally, it will be helpful to your progress if you find a partner or a small group with which to study and practice Sat Nam Rasayan. You will be able to take turns reading the practice instructions to each other and also take turns being healer and client.

Sat Nam Rasayan is very simple. It is a specific and clearly defined state of awareness that happens in your neutral, meditative, mind. All spiritual traditions teach how to reach one or more particular spiritual or sacred states. In order to learn Sat Nam Rasayan all you need to do is to recognize when you are in this particular Sacred Space and then become able to hold yourself stable in it. It is not so difficult or uncommon to briefly experience spiritual or meditative states. Most people with a regular spiritual practice have had at least fleeting glimpses of states of relatively elevated awareness or spiritual consciousness, and you should be able to do that with Sat Nam Rasayan as well. But it is more rare to be able to sustain the experience over a few minutes, and rarer still to be able to maintain such consciousness during everyday activities. Your Sat Nam Rasayan practice, guided by the exercises in this book, will be directed at this stability. Through practice you will gain an ever-greater capacity to maintain yourself in an intimate and intense relationship with the experience of this moment.

A basic healing session with Sat Nam Rasayan is often a most undramatic affair. A few words may be exchanged as the client tells the healer of his or her concerns, although this is not really necessary. The client then lies down and the healer sits in meditation next to the client. Both can be seated in chairs if that is easier. For now, the only criteria are that both the client and the healer be comfortable, and that the healer be able to lightly touch the arm of the client. Then, to an outside observer, nothing else would appear to happen until the healing session is over. After the session there might be some conversation as the healer gives the client suggestions for further work. The entire session could last anywhere from a few minutes up to an hour or so, depending on the experience of the healer, the complexity of the problems being worked on, how many issues are being addressed, the resistance of the client, and so on.

The inner process of healing as experienced by the client might also be undramatic. Most typically the experience is of deep relaxation or even a trancelike sleep, although sometimes there are obvious releases of held tension with the client feeling new energy or a deeper breathing pattern. After healing sessions clients may need just a little time to become fully alert and ready to go about normal activities.

The healer's experience is what is most unique about Sat Nam Rasayan. He or she will be engaged in the sensitive process or will be established in the Sacred Space. In the healer there will be great sensitivity—the particular kind of sensitivity that you will be learning about here. The healer remains neutral—that is, allows, without prejudice or resistance, whatever he or she experiences. This itself is very healing, as you will soon understand from firsthand experience, but the healer may then also make additional subtle movements in his or her consciousness in order to more efficiently release the chronic tendencies in the client that have caused the difficulties. The rest of this book will show you how all of this is possible.

This book will not prepare you to work in a professional relationship with clients, although you will certainly be prepared to work personally with friends and family. If you are already a healing professional or a minister or counselor, what is taught here can be incorporated into your practice in the same way that any other new ideas or knowledge or insights might be. This book will not teach you to diagnose illness or prescribe treatments. Any advice that you might want to give to a client after a healing session should be recognized as your personal intuition, not as professional recommendations. If you are already a healing professional, the wisdom derived from Sat Nam Rasayan will find its natural and rightful place in your discussions with patients.

Sat Nam Rasayan can, in fact, be used along with any other healing technique. Whether a healer uses acupuncture or surgery, herbs or chemotherapy, patients are well served when the healer operates, at least part of the time, from either the sensitive space or the Sacred Space of Sat Nam Rasayan. This infuses the healing with an underlying sensitivity and understanding not normally available, and enhances whatever other techniques are being used. And yet Sat Nam Rasayan is not just a supplement to other healing. It is more fundamental than that. Sat Nam Rasayan is what healers in other disciplines should know to help them to master their methods and their lives. It provides a foundation of intuition, awareness, compassion, and love, and makes these qualities not only philosophically desirable but also attainable through specific practices.

Love, for example, is the quality of unconditional acceptance, not the culmination of an ever-increasing affection for another. True love can only result from the practice of fearlessness, of fearlessly allowing into one's consciousness whatever might appear there when one is in relation to another. Understood in this way, love becomes an art that can be practiced and mastered, a state totally beyond preferences or personality. Regardless of your personal feelings or the way that another presents him- or herself to you, if you are fully able to allow within you the sensations that appear when you are in relation to that person, your relation can be loving and nonjudgmental. When you have practiced and learned this loving quality, it will be a part of your presence, your healing, and your life. Similarly, intuition, compassion, and awareness are arts that can be learned. Each will develop in proportion to your capacity to allow the experience of this moment, a capacity that can be expanded through practice. Thus, these most treasured of human traits, these qualities of higher consciousness, can be cultivated and attained by absolutely everyone who has the will to excel.

You will learn all this through the sensitive process. This process is simple in theory and easy enough to understand, but it will take practice to master. The practice, however, is a delight in itself and very rewarding. If you are already established in a meditative practice, the sensitive process will help you to deepen that practice. If you are newer to meditation and are a bit unsure of yourself, the sensitive process will help you immensely as you learn to meditate. And, if you have never meditated, the sensitive process will get you started in an excellent way.

The Sat Nam Rasayan healing art is unique in that it uses only the healer's awareness and no other tools or forces. In Gurmukhi, the sacred language of the Sikhs, *Sat* means "truth," *Nam* means "name" or "identity," and *Rasayan* refers to "deep relaxation" or "an elixir." Thus *Sat Nam Rasayan* means "to rejuvenate through an awareness of the true, divine, nature of being." It is a way of being deeply aware, so that one can be highly efficient and effective at healing oneself or another. It is not a substitute for the medicines or manipulations that a health practitioner might apply in an attempt to bring about a cure; when those forces are necessary they should also be used. Sat Nam Rasayan works on a different level. It uses your meditative mind and your ability to transcend everyday consciousness to enhance the inner environment of healing, helping to release conditions that might have led to illness in the first place, or that might keep a patient from recovering. It can sometimes appear that Sat Nam Rasayan has brought about an almost miraculous recovery, but it is the healing capacity of human beings that is miraculous, not any individual healer. All the healer has done is to help release resistance. The client, and God within the client, has done the healing.

This book will guide you in how to practice the sensitive process that Guru Dev has developed. Throughout the book there are brief instructions for practice sessions, some done by yourself and some done with a partner. Take time for these practices, and repeat them often. This is not a book that needs to be read in a short time. Take several months to go through it, practicing all the while, and return to it from time to time as your experience develops. Practice is all-important. This is a book about experience: your experience. Put in a half-hour or more each day, in addition to your other spiritual practice, or your progress may be slow.

As you become proficient in serving others through the practice of Sat Nam Rasayan, you will notice that the practice has, as a side effect, an enormous benefit to you as a healer. Sat Nam Rasayan is for healing but it is also undeniably a most powerful spiritual practice. You will soon find yourself enjoying deeper, more blissful meditations. You will find yourself more loving, more aware, more sensitive in all aspects of your life, and more able to deal with whatever discomfort and challenge you face. But all of these are side effects and not our primary purpose. Our purpose is to heal. The practices that I will be suggesting to you will challenge you to suspend some of your old ways of thinking and to open yourself to a nonrational transcendent consciousness. As you use this process it will bring you closer and closer to a state of transcendence—a pure, direct knowing, with the capacity to modify an event solely with your consciousness, for the purposes of healing.

As you study Sat Nam Rasayan you will find that there is not too much to learn, and nothing whatsoever to memorize, but there is a good deal to practice. Some parts of this book will seem quite clear to you while others, at first, may not. After going through the book once, reread sections in any order. Put in extra practice time with the parts that remain confusing. When you are confused please understand that you are more than intelligent enough to excel at healing, but that a limitation of any book is that it is not a workshop or a class where a teacher can respond directly to your questions and guide your practice. I have tried to anticipate your questions and have approached some topic areas in several different ways, hoping that at least one of my approaches will speak to you. Go ahead now and begin your studies. I hope this book will serve you well.

THE ESSENCE
OF HEALING

AWARENESS, balance, happiness, peace, and flexibility are all essentials of healing, just as they are among the essentials of a life well lived. Healing, as we will be using the word, does not mean simply the elimination of disease—that is what we will call a cure. Healing has a more exalted meaning than that. In the language of Sat Nam Rasayan, healing happens when one releases or corrects conditions that have produced harmful tendencies or patterns, whether these tendencies have led to frank disease or not. Thus, healing can occur before there is disease. When disease has occurred it will be eliminated when the release of these conditions happens early enough for the body to recover. One who is healed has an ability to remain relaxed and peaceful in the face of difficulties, and has the flexibility to adapt to changing and difficult conditions in an appropriate, healthful way.

We can always choose to fight back against illness, but to demand or even hope that there be no illness (or no failures in life, or no strife) is to foolishly fly in the face of the inevitable, attempting to force our will where we are bound to fail, struggling with a foe that cannot be beaten. In this there can be no peace. A saner, healthier approach is to learn to fight our battles without losing our ability to accept what is.

If in this moment I have cancer, then that is something I can seek to make peace with even as I search for a cure. But curing my disease and healing my life and spirit might very well remain two separate and distinct processes. I may eventually be cured but not healed, or healed but not cured.

Curing is the application of some energy so as to encourage a person into a pattern of greater health. The surgeon's knife, the herbalist's remedy, the chiropractor's adjustment, the psychic's manipulation of the energy field of a chakra— these are all ways of curing. There is an external agent in each of these, and an individual in the role of practitioner (although one may treat oneself). To be effective the treatment must augment the patient's natural and inherent tendency to return to health. An infection, for example, can be treated and cured with an antibiotic, but the drug is effective only insofar as it supports and enhances natural healing processes.

Healing is the process going on behind the scenes during a cure, the silent hero that empowers the remedy, the modification of the conditions that led to disease in the first place. Without the cooperation of the body's and mind's powerful urges toward health, our methods of care and cure would seem pathetic indeed. When the mysterious forces of healing cannot be marshaled, the patient does not recover. Chemotherapy, surgery, and radiation treatments may destroy a tumor, but if a single cancer cell remains and the body is unable to destroy it on its own, with its own healing forces, then the cancer may return, the remission will be over, and the patient may die. Here is where you, as healer, can have your influence. You may or may not already be a health care professional, a purveyor of cures, but you can be a healer in either case, and through awareness modify harmful tendencies in your client.

The Essence of Healing

Healing is mysterious and is likely to remain so. Why does one person recover and another die? What yearning causes a cell to snub a noxious chemical? How is it that a long depression may finally lift? Science may give us partial answers to questions like these, but I doubt if a complete unraveling of these enigmas is possible. The inner healing process is often perfectly adequate for complete recovery, even in the absence of any attempts at a cure. We are all familiar with our own healing powers, having healed from minor cuts and bruises that required no treatment. We routinely recover from colds and other minor viral and bacterial infections, without any outside help. Even more serious traumas and illnesses often heal without treatment. Emotional healing is also possible without professional help. The loss of one's spouse, one of the most difficult emotional traumas, may require a long period of healing, but we generally expect that such healing will eventually come to pass. This is the miracle of healing —miraculous in the same way that life itself is miraculous: partially, but never completely, understandable.

Healing obviously benefits from a supportive environment. If I cut my arm and have it stitched and bandaged and change the dressings regularly, healing will most likely proceed uneventfully. If I had no way to clean and stitch the wound and no bandages to protect it, healing might not happen so smoothly. My arm could get infected, the infection could spread, it could threaten my life. Even if I eventually recovered, my arm might be scarred, and I might end up with limited use of it. In the case of one who has lost a loved one, he or she may never heal and return to happiness without the support of friends and family, or in the absence of sound mental health to begin with. We all know of people who have never fully recovered from emotional trauma.

Beyond this physical and emotional healing there is also

the healing of the spirit, the healing of life itself, but there are, of course, no ways of really separating these different aspects of healing. Emotional health is vital to physical healing and spiritual peace; physical health is conducive to emotional health and spiritual balance, and so on. But the healing of a life needs to be considered separately for one simple reason: we are all going to die. Sooner or later, our physical health will fail. It may fail instantly as in a serious accident, or it may fail over a long period of time due to a slowly progressing illness, but it must fail and we must die. When we do, that death need not be understood simply as the final failure of the body. Death can also be a time for the triumph of the spirit. If during life there has been healing, an accumulation of wisdom, patience, compassion, and self-confidence, the end of life can be a time of abiding peace. Healing of the spirit is like mental and physical healing in that it can happen without outside help, but like emotional and physical healing, spiritual healing flourishes best in a supportive environment. A strong spiritual practice or membership in a community of like-minded brothers and sisters is of inestimable value if we are to hope for spiritual healing and inner peace.

Healing is an ongoing process. Its primary purpose is not to simply rid us of disease or other difficulty or to thoroughly smooth our way. Rather, healing is the work of coming into balance with whatever our current circumstances may be. Illness or health, peace or war, love or fear—whatever the inner or outer conditions may be, healing is possible because healing is not the correction of our conditions but rather the return to balance and peace. If our view is that some condition of our life is wrong and it must be fixed before we can feel whole and at peace again, then we are condemning ourselves to a sort of victimhood, with life and all of its vicissitudes as persecutors, because only rarely are all the conditions of life going to be as we would have them. How often can we hope that everything will go our way? "Perfect" conditions are the exception rather than the rule, and waiting for perfection, or working toward it, can consume both our days and our energy. Certainly, there is effort to be made, wrongs to right, and diseases to cure, but there is other "work" that also needs doing and that is the humble work of healing. This effortless play of healing (for it certainly is no work at all) consists simply of fearlessly allowing ourselves to experience whatever is happening at this moment. When we can do that, a miracle happens—the miracle of healing.

One need not be physically or mentally ill, in need, that is, of a cure, before embarking on a healing journey. In fact, cures may be impossible, and still we can heal. For healing is, above all else, a matter of the spirit. It is how we gain in tolerance, how we handle the physical and mental traumas of life. It is an inner process of remembering and acknowledging our inherent completeness as we let go of the need to protect ourselves through patterned, inflexible responses to life's challenges. Wounds heal as the body "remembers" its natural state. A mind heals when a victim of childhood sexual abuse regains her ability to laugh and play as she did before the abuse began—when she remembers her joyful, unhurt, and unafraid self. Lives heal as we recapture our capacity to fearlessly guide ourselves toward fulfillment and satisfying engagement with others. And spirit heals as we recall and move closer to a sense of our own divine nature, toward a fuller merging with God and nature, toward happiness, flexibility, and inner peace.

Sat Nam Rasayan is effective for reasons that do not necessarily make sense to the rational mind. When you are in the presence of someone who is peaceful, or angry, or who has a great deal of personal power, you can feel that. His or her presence has an effect on you. You've experienced that and you know it is true, but can you explain why it is so? If you fell and hurt yourself you could explain that—you tripped, fell, struck your knee, stimulated the nerve endings in a certain way, caused some inflammation, and so on. The result is pain and a limitation of movement for a few days. This is understandable. But our experience of the presence of another is not so easy to explain. We know it happens but we can't say how.

Real understanding of the potential healing power of your presence will come out of your direct experience, and that, as I have said, is only going to happen with practice. Suspend any disbelief you might have and assume for now that transcendence is possible. Assume that it is possible (however briefly) to step outside the material universe and experience some of what is normally altogether beyond the bounds of human cognition. Assume further that consciousness is able to effect change and that intentions in the consciousness can modify events. If you can make these assumptions then you are well on your way to understanding Sat Nam Rasayan. Sat Nam Rasayan is simply the state in which a healer transcends everyday consciousness, becomes aware of the consciousness in an event, and modifies that event so as to allow healing. Begin by embracing the concept that you do, in fact, affect others with your presence. What you will be learning is how to do that intentionally and for the purposes of healing.

You are a healer. It is in your nature to be able to develop your capacity to bring yourself into a neutral, meditative state and in that state have a profoundly positive effect on yourself, on other people, and on your environment in general. We all have this potential. You have the capacity to facilitate the natural healing capacity in others and help them to return to a state of balance and happiness.

The Essence of Healing

This is no small thing. There is so much suffering in the world. Cancer, AIDS, and other terrible diseases are all around us. Economic uncertainty and the curse of poverty cause enormous stress and tension. Environmental disasters and political and social unrest are enough to frighten any thinking person. This is a time for people to reestablish their own balance and to reach into their hearts to serve those in need.

These essentials of healing, the capacity to modify or release a condition that has caused and sustained a harmful tendency, along with the qualities of intuition, compassion, consciousness, and love, when coupled with the intention to heal, can well stand alone, without any other techniques, as a full-fledged healing art. Thus, through your presence, you can act as an effective healer. No matter what your background, whether you are a highly trained physician or have no particular healing experience, Sat Nam Rasayan, the essence of healing, is for everyone because everyone, potentially, is a healer.

Although we will use the sensitive process in order to learn Sat Nam Rasayan, the sensitive process is just a teaching tool, and ultimately it will be left behind like the training wheels of your first bicycle. This is because Sat Nam Rasayan is a state of consciousness rather than a technique; it is more about your awareness and your presence than it is about anything else. These aspects of you, awareness and presence, can be cultivated and nurtured, but like transcendence, they cannot be forced. No sequence of steps, no instructions, regardless of how carefully they may be followed, can ever teach you the essence of Sat Nam Rasayan. That, you can only learn through your own direct experience, which in turn you can only obtain through practice.

BECOMING
NEUTRAL

N EUTRALITY is the fundamental quality that allows one to become transcendent and then modify an event that occurs in awareness. It is what allows you to release the conditions that have held you or a client in harmful, habitual patterns or tendencies. If you were meditating and your foot became uncomfortable, your "tendency" might be to concentrate attention on your sore foot, limiting the awareness available for other things. Or you might move your foot, but this would only serve to reinforce the preconception or "condition" in your consciousness that says a sore foot is undesirable and is to be avoided. You must be stable in your meditation in order to become neutral and release conditions. This stability is the state in which there is no concentration, no focus on any one thing, no reactivity, and yet it is a state in which every sensation that is experienced is allowed to be, equally with all other sensations. No one sensation, no matter how intense it might be, is given more attention than any other sensation.

If you wish to heal with the sensitive process, you will need to work in a neutral way with whatever appears in your consciousness, including discomfort and difficulties. We are used to concentrating on whatever irritates us, and we are forever fighting with our pains and fears. But we must begin our healing practice now by providing a space in which, in the face of discomfort or distraction, we do nothing. This doesn't mean that you have to hold onto your mind very tightly, restricting it like a police officer holding down a violent criminal, because then your mind's energy would come back at you, and the struggle would just continue in a new form. Nor does this imply that you need to become so loose that you let go of your mind completely, because then it will just become wild and chaotic. Instead you need to let your mind go but within a particular kind of discipline, and within a particular set of guidelines. The aim is for you to soften your resistance and allow yourself to feel the sensations of experience.

✄ TUNE IN AND OPEN THE SENSITIVE SPACE

For your first practice exercise, simply sit now, in a dignified meditation posture. Aim for a posture that allows you to be relaxed and comfortable yet erect and alert. You can sit cross-legged on the floor, with or without a cushion for support, or you can sit straight on a firm chair. Sat Nam Rasayan doesn't require a particular sitting position, but at this stage in your practice any of the common meditation postures will be helpful in keeping you alert and aware. You don't want to become drowsy nor do you want to be overly bothered by aching knees or sore neck muscles.

Close your eyes and "tune in." Tuning in is an aspect of spiritual practice that I especially want to encourage you to use. Before beginning your healing or meditation practice, pause and declare in your consciousness that this time will be devoted to the sacred, the divine, the boundless. The method of tuning in that Yogi Bhajan has taught begins with bringing the palms of your hands together at

Becoming Neutral

the center of your chest, as if to pray, and then taking a deep in-
halation and chanting aloud "Ong Namo." Then take a quicker
inhalation and chant "Guru Dev Namo," with each phrase taking
about ten seconds to chant. Then repeat the entire process two more
times. The musical notation for this chant is

ONG   NA MO   GURU DEV   NA MO

The chant is demonstrated on the audiotape that comes with my
book Meditation for Absolutely Everyone.

"Ong" *is a reference to the Creator that exists in all things.*
"Namo" *is a humble bow to that Creator.* "Guru Dev" *refers to the*
divine wisdom of the Infinite, and "Namo" *again is a recognition of*
its greatness. Taken together, the implication is that we are now set-
ting aside our personal, ego-driven self in favor of the unlimited
universal intelligence that can flow through us. It is a powerful way
to begin. In this book I will remind you to tune in before each exer-
cise, but it isn't necessary to tune in more than once in each prac-
tice session, even if you are doing several exercises in that session.

So, having tuned in, gradually become aware of whatever sensa-
tions you are experiencing in your body at this moment. Feel the air
on your skin. Feel the pressure of your legs against your cushion or
chair. Feel the breath moving through your nostrils and the expan-
sion and contraction of your lungs with each breath. Feel sensations
of tension and relaxation and sensations of discomfort and plea-
sure. Feel the pull of gravity against different parts of your body.
Take your time and continually expand your consciousness so that
you can feel more and more.

Also feel the more subtle, small, quiet sensations between the
more obvious ones. Feel sensations that have no particular name.
Take your time and allow still more sensations into your awareness.

If you are having thoughts, recognize the sensations that are associated with those thoughts and allow them as well, without any hint of judgment. You may wish you weren't thinking, or were more comfortable, but just notice what that wish feels like in you and what the thoughts feel like, and don't concern yourself with how well you are doing.

If you are aware of outside stimuli, noises or smells, for example, notice the sensations that arise in relation to them. It may not be obvious at first but you will soon recognize that your experience of a sound or a smell is not of the thing that has created the sound or smell but of sensations somewhere in your body (usually not in your nose or ears) that arise in response to it. Be aware of these, again without judgment. There are, for our purposes, no good sensations and no bad sensations, and all should be allowed equally.

Continue to meditate in this way for fifteen minutes or more. There is no rush. If you feel frustrated just open your eyes for a moment, close them, and begin the practice again. When you are done, notice how you feel, and how the practice has affected you.

As you do this practice you will be relating to nothing more and nothing less than the experience of this moment. Out of this practice, things that have been hidden away in nooks and crannies at the bottom of your mind may rise to the surface. This is a good thing, as it will enable you to witness the subtle effects of whatever you have been avoiding. The experience could be intense at first, but if you simply allow the intense feelings, without trying to solve anything just now, you will see that these feelings lose their power. Whenever I help a student or a client to simply be present with long suppressed feelings, there is always a relief of the intensity. Emotions and thoughts, and more importantly the sensations that are experienced in relation to them, should be neither suppressed nor indulged but simply allowed to be. If you are sad, let the feelings of sadness touch you, and feel their touch. If you are hurting, let that touch you. If you feel pleasure, allow that sensation to touch you.

Meditation in Sat Nam Rasayan is the absolute allowing of our own inner environment and the actual experience of this moment. When we do this we develop an openness to the environment outside of ourselves. If we are not judging our inner experience, then we will not judge the outer experience that gives rise to the inner. Then we are able to know things as they are, without worrying about how to hold onto our experience or how it could be improved upon. This acceptance of inner and outer conditions is the beginning of genuine love and compassion, and these, in turn, are the essence of healing.

As you practice in this way, over a period of months, you will notice not only a new ability as a healer but also an ever-increasing ability to handle the stresses of your own life. You will begin to recognize that the difficulty and pain you face are not so bad in and of themselves, but are only hard to endure if there is a strong urge to avoid the feelings and sensations that arise in you in response to those difficulties and pains. As you learn to allow your sensations you will find that suffering is reduced, and life will take on new richness and ease.

We consume a good deal of energy by our desire to avoid pain or to increase pleasure. More often than not our urge for comfort appears as a barely conscious drive over which we have little control. At a recent workshop Ruth (not her real name) asked question after question, dominating the discussions. After several hours of this, another participant I'll call Alan angrily interrupted her. He complained of her taking too much of the group's time and of not being considerate of others' needs. When I asked Alan to pay attention to what he was feeling, he recognized an unpleasant tension in his abdomen. When I asked him if he could recall when he first felt this way, Alan began to talk of his overly controlling mother. As a child he had not been able to express his feelings around his mother and he had learned to avoid his feelings, which he now felt as the tension bottled up in his abdomen. At the workshop, or presumably whenever he was with someone who reminded him of his mother's difficult traits, Alan became tense. To avoid simply being present with his own sensations, he chose to be angry instead. By becoming angry Alan put the responsibility for his feelings far outside of himself, and lost touch with his own sensations of tension. For four decades controlling people had made him angry. What is most remarkable is that in the few minutes it took to become clear about all of this, Alan's feelings of tension and anger were replaced by a sense of peacefulness and relaxation.

Turning my attention to Ruth, I asked her to recall the sensations in her body just as she was about to ask one of her questions. She was able to identify a set of feelings that she summarized with the word "empty." She recalled how empty she had felt growing up and how, even in the first grade, she had learned to fill her empty place by "taking it all in." Ruth seldom really felt her emptiness, choosing instead to demand her teachers' attentions, even though the pleasure of filling herself in that way must have had some negative social consequences, as it had in our workshop. Her domineering ways, like Alan's anger, kept her out of touch with her actual experience. As with Alan, as soon as she spent a little time with her long-suppressed feelings she began to relax.

Becoming Neutral

The feelings of both Alan and Ruth were not so horrible or compelling after all, they were just feelings, sensations that they were quite capable of working with, once they were allowed. Later in the workshop, when Ruth had another question, she asked it in a way that showed sensitivity both to her own feelings and to everyone else's and, when she was speaking, Alan didn't keep his back to her as he had all morning, but instead turned toward Ruth, able to be genuinely interested in what she was saying.

We need to recognize when we are avoiding unpleasant sensations (as Alan did with his tension) or when we are seeking still more of the pleasant sensations that we have become addicted to (as Ruth did when she tried to fill herself with my attention). As we do this we develop our "presence," our capacity to remain neutral in the face of the difficult or the enticing, without reacting blindly to either. Faced with people we consider difficult we are able to see them as they really are—just people trying to ease their own pain. By allowing our own discomfort in their presence, we can, by extension, allow them to feel discomfort. This is the beginning of love and compassion. This is the beginning of being able to "be there" for others and to serve their need for loving attention.

These same phenomena often take on a different flavor. I know, for example, many men and women who have learned to cover their feelings of aloneness with flirtatious behavior. They work hard to be attractive. Even though some might consider their behavior pleasant, it is still patterned behavior hiding their real feelings. And just as Alan's anger at Ruth's pattern was itself a pattern, so the target of flirtation is likely to reply with his or her own pattern, whether it be of attraction or repulsion. In either case, the reaction may be covering deeper feelings of neediness or fear of intimacy. It is only when we allow ourselves to get close to our own experience, without reactivity, that we can begin to become free of such automatic responses. It is then that we can be present for others, then that we can make clear decisions about what to do in any given situation, then that we can begin to love and serve in a pure way, not for selfish gratification but for joyful fulfillment.

Before reading further, practice more with the meditation exercise *Tune In and Open the Sensitive Space*, described earlier. There is no magic formula for learning to heal, only this need to practice. Ask yourself what you are trying to achieve. Is it not to reduce your fears and suffering and to help others to do so as well? Is it not to be happy and to reduce the dissatisfaction, separation, loneliness, and insecurity in you and in those you know? Diligent practice with Sat Nam Rasayan will help you do so.

LETTING GO
OF SELF

THE WORK we are doing is actually quite simple, although we complicate it unnecessarily. We are saddled with a compulsion to serve and protect our ego-self, all that we call "I," "me," or "mine." But that effort is largely unnecessary. The true self is quite safe. That self, the soul, has never been hurt, has never been in need of healing. It has always remained pure and untouched by the difficulties of life. But we forget, we sleep, and we dream another reality, of suffering and desire.

What we seek to protect actually has no reality outside of our own minds. From birth we have been accumulating ideas about our selves and about the world. We have endless concepts and prejudices about what is desirable, what is to be avoided, what sort of person is attractive, whom we should be afraid of, and so on. We also have endless ideas about ourselves: what we are like, what we are good at, what threatens us, and what others think of us. All of this is just belief, derived from how we have learned to interpret our experience. Had our experience or our interpretations been different, we would have a different sense of self. So there is nothing absolute about this personal self; it is our own creation and has only a limited existence outside of our minds. But the issues of attraction to one thing and avoidance of another seem so important that we become completely wrapped up in them. We forget who we were before accumulating our self-concepts. We forget our original self.

In this sense our belief in the personal self as a distinct entity is an illusion, a side effect that arises because our original self lies temporarily hidden within a human form. It is the human body and mind that is vulnerable and needs protection from the elements; it is not the soul. In our effort to protect out vulnerable self, we spend virtually all of our energy optimizing our experience. We fear one thing and desire another and devote our lives to having it our way. Obviously we would not have survived as a species if we didn't do this, but we have done it at an enormous cost. The cost is that we have fallen asleep and live in a dream world in which the mental and physical are the only realities that we perceive. In this dream, we see ourselves and others as distinct and separate beings in need of protection. The task now is to awaken to the other reality, that of the God in all.

A beginning of the awakening, and the clarity and ease that the awakening implies, occurs when we engage in the practice of letting go of our point of view, that reference point that would have us believe that we exist here. When that is accomplished we can let go of the urge to control our experience and instead we can begin to let our experience touch us directly. When we let go of our egocentric point of view we develop a tremendous opportunity to allow our experience to occur without resistance. Whatever happens in the vast space of ego-free awareness, be it pleasure or pain, sickness or health, birth or death, we can then allow and experience it in its fullness.

Be absolutely clear about this. It is not that sickness no

longer matters, or that we can simply allow ourselves to die without looking for a cure. The body and mind do need to be cared for and protected, and there is ample reason for us to prefer pleasure to pain, but if we feel pain and we are unable to remain present with it, or if we feel pleasure and we are unable to fully experience it or are desirous of still more, then we are resisting our actual experience. In that case, we are shutting out a part of what is, a part of the reality that we call God. When, on the other hand, we allow the experience of this moment, despite our preferences, that experience can touch the tender heart of us, and it will enlighten us.

Unfortunately we usually put up defenses against much of our experience, and our heart remains encased in armor. We have been hurt, physically and emotionally, and not every wound received all the attention it needed for full healing. That is inevitable. We then learned patterned ways to avoid similar wounds. A simple example: Richard, one of my clients, grew up in a family where there was little demonstration of love, and with parents who allowed Richard's older sister to tease him mercilessly. The pain of the teasing was more than he could bear, and he escaped from his sister by hiding himself away, alone in his room. There, the pain of being alone was almost unbearable and Richard would spend hours desperately wishing for his mother to come to him and soothe him, but she never did. As an adult, married and with his own family, Richard continued to feel isolated from the affection he desired. He had come to believe that he was always going to be alone, and he was extremely sensitive to any withholding of affection.

Richard established several lines of defense against the threat of having to feel once again the pain of loneliness. The first defense was anger. If his wife didn't comfort him when he was upset he was quick to anger (which tended to push her away and increase his sense of isolation). As he worked against this pattern he came to the next line of defense, closer in. When he let the anger drop away, he felt instead the more fundamental desire for comfort. But at this level he was essentially saying, "I'm not angry but I am alone and that is the way it will always be. It's not worth trying to get what I want. I might as well go off and live by myself." To do so would have re-created the scene in his bedroom—alone and desperate for someone to come to him. With further work, Richard was able to let down this second line of defense. When he did, he felt not the desperation, but something even more central, the fear of isolation. Further effort brought him beyond the fear of isolation to the feeling itself. This is what he had spent a lifetime trying to avoid with his fear and desire and anger. But then a remarkable thing happened. When Richard finally allowed himself to feel what he had been at such pains to avoid, the feeling turned out to be just a feeling—a sort of pressure in the center of his chest. He found that he was able to tolerate that feeling quite well. When he simply allowed it to be there, without any avoidance or resistance, things began to change almost immediately. The sense that this was a pain to be avoided at all costs (even at the cost of anger at his wife, or living alone) began to dissipate. The feeling in his chest slowly evaporated and in its place there was a sense of peace. As a child, things were quite different. Then, being isolated was literally life threatening, and even though Richard was never physically neglected, his feeling of being alone was truly terrifying. As an adult, he certainly knew that he was physically safe, but the pattern had been established and simple reason had little effect. Only by experiencing what he was fearful of could the healing begin.

Letting Go of Self

Everything naturally changes; nothing remains the same. For Richard, or any of us, to be stuck in a pattern means that there is a good deal of energy going into keeping things the way they have always been. Releasing defenses is how we can stop the hard work of holding things the same. When we do, conditions will change and our evolution can continue. The central element in all of what Richard learned to do was awareness and allowing experience to touch him. In Sat Nam Rasayan it is the particular sort of awareness that we call "allowing." It is the awareness that includes no judgment, no resistance, and no concentration—an awareness that permits things to be exactly as they are and allows us to experience reality without resistance. This is how we grow and it is also how we heal others.

It will challenge you to learn to be aware in this particular way. The need is to cut through the ego's fears and desires and its ambition to maintain its own safe and separate existence. In Sat Nam Rasayan you are asked to release some of your most basic assumptions about what is safe and what is real. Instead, allow what is real, namely the sensations and experience of this moment, to happen to you. Try not to be concerned with the individual self that you have always defended. Instead, drop the "point of view" and recognize that the consciousness you currently call "you" is in no way different from the universal consciousness that exists everywhere, in all things and in all people. The consciousness that is manifested in you is fundamentally the same consciousness that is manifested in the client you are treating, regardless of the superficial differences and the illusion of separateness.

As you practice and refine your healing work, your practice will lead you to realize that there is no need for, and no advantage to, holding onto your beliefs or concepts about experiences. This is very liberating. This is how you can let go of clinging to old habit patterns, and instead fearlessly approach new and unfamiliar experience. Before this you may have preferred the safe and secure prison of your concepts to the freedom of release. You may have remained absorbed in belief systems because they felt safer than the uncertainties they hid: the ego's nagging fear that, without vigilance, it (and you) could cease to exist.

Don't expect this radical change to happen all at once, that you may suddenly be perfectly stable in the Space, empty of your conditions and free of ego. But once you have explored and become comfortable in the Space even a little, your progress will accelerate. You will become quieter and more stable, and it will happen fast. Others who enter into similar spaces for the purposes of enlightenment may take years to progress as far as you will in a few months if your purpose is healing. The link of spiritual practice to service is a great accelerator. You will, of course, apply the lessons of Sat Nam Rasayan outside of the healing environment and they will enlighten your life. But that is not our primary purpose. The purpose is to heal, and the enlightenment that may come to you is purely a delightful side effect.

When you are in the position of healer, remember that it is not you who heals. The healer is consciousness, not your consciousness but consciousness itself. There is no healing without the Sacred Space, and it is the lineage that holds the Space. It has been the school of Sat Nam Rasayan, the teachers of Sat Nam Rasayan, and their ability to hold the Space that have combined with your practice with the sensitive process to induce in you your experience of the Sacred Space. That is what has taught you to make the jump from the normal to the Sacred. Don't think, "I am doing this" or "I have taught myself to heal," as that is a formula for pain and failure. Just produce a little space within yourself, a place that is not filled with ego's beliefs, concepts, and judgments, and then let there be freedom and healing in that space. Acknowledge where this capacity you have has come from, honor the lineage and the way that it is working through you. You will become more and more aware. With your awareness you will be serving another, and so your progress will be quick. The lovely irony is that in the moment you give up your desire for healing power, you will have it. Power in Sat Nam Rasayan comes only with the intensity of your desire to give up your power and to be in a position of service.

RELEASING
CONDITIONS

I N SAT NAM RASAYAN we do not give recipes for how to treat this condition or that. I won't tell you that certain feelings or sensations you may experience mean particular things about your client or that they require a particular response on your part. If I were to do that, assuming that I could, you would then have a head full of information and might have the tendency to try to fit the poor client into your preconceived notions, putting her, as it were, into a box that was not necessarily her size. So I will just tell you that what you need to know is what you already do know: your own experience. Just learn to recognize your sensations in the space of the relation with your client or partner. As you do this work you will gradually develop the ability to translate what you feel into intelligible information. You will be able to tell your clients what is wrong, and how it came to be as it is, and how they might help themselves. Long before you have that ability you will be able to heal with your capacity to release tension and anxiety and bring a more natural and healthful balance to your clients. You will be in a relation with a client and recognize a sensation of contraction in youself, and you will release that sensation in an act no more complex than casually scratching an itch. Even if you are never able to explain this it won't matter; you will still be healing.

43

One risky part of Sat Nam Rasayan is trying to translate what we feel into everyday language. We can feel with great sensitivity and precision, but may translate only poorly, without precision, misinterpreting the meaning of our experience. So allow the ability to translate to come along slowly and don't pay too much attention to it in the beginning. What we care about now is learning to release the contractions or conditions that hold the tendencies that make the client sick.

⚔ ALLOW SENSATIONS

Once again, tune in and sit in meditation. Close your eyes and repeat the process of becoming aware of all of your sensations, without discrimination. Allow into your awareness whatever might appear there. Include everything that appears but concentrate on none of it. Take your time with this. Not concentrating on any one sensation will gradually lead you to an equal awareness of all sensations.

When you feel that you have an equal awareness of all the sensations in your body, select from among them a single sensation, the one that is most uncomfortable. Don't concentrate on this one sensation but remain aware of it along with everything else. Recognize the resistance that you may have to this sensation and allow the sensations of that resistance, also without any concentration.

Continue to allow all sensations, including any new ones that may appear, while keeping the discomfort (and the sensations of the resistance to the discomfort) in your awareness as well. Continue in this way until the discomfort is resolved.

In this exercise, you might have noticed, for example, some stiffness in your neck. Normally you might have shifted your position, but here you will just notice the sensations of the stiffness. You might also tend to resist the feeling of the stiffness and experience that resistance as some tightening felt in your stomach or as a heavy feeling in your face. You are being asked here to recognize those sensations as well, but not to react to them. This exercise should lead to a decrease in the sensation of discomfort. All that is necessary is that you be aware, without judgment.

Our usual approach to pain is to attempt to block it out or to try to escape it in some other way, as Richard did with his feelings of loneliness. But that process is itself painful and can have many negative consequences. Sometimes we are in pain and sometimes we have escaped pain, and alternating between the two states is also difficult. Here, in our healing work, we are doing something radically different. Here, we are saying that pain is allowed, exactly as we would allow a neutral feeling such as the pull of gravity on the skin of our arm. Here, there is no judging, and that is a radical departure for most of us. But that is the simple essence of healing others and of healing our own lives. Without this neutral view of our discomfort, we can feel no peace, and it is this peace, this neutral, aware presence, that we are cultivating with Sat Nam Rasayan. This is not to suggest that in life one ought to give up one's preferences, or choose to avoid pain when pain is a useful warning signal. The master of Sat Nam Rasayan does not casually touch a hot frying pan or choose to spend time with angry people without good reason. But the practice of Sat Nam Rasayan does give us the capacity to remain neutral in the face of difficult experience. Whether we then choose to remain in contact with the people or conditions that led to the difficult experience is a matter of personal choice. Sometimes it is better to face these circumstances; sometimes it is better to turn away. Only with a neutral mind can the choice be a truly free one.

Obviously, our healing work is very different from the

work of other kinds of health practitioners. The practice of Sat Nam Rasayan consists of creating and maintaining a stable meditative presence and in that state entering into an intentional relation with a client, or with a particular aspect of a client, with the intention to heal through that Sacred, meditative state. This is different from using a meditative state to enhance intuition and then using intuitive understanding to design a treatment plan. It is different from treating a client with channeled energy. It is certainly different from gathering facts and observations about a patient and concluding from them that a particular disease is present and a certain treatment is called for. Sat Nam Rasayan is a good deal more direct and simple than any of these.

In Sat Nam Rasayan it is almost as if there were no patient at all, just the healer, fully present with his or her own experience. Imagine sitting in meditation, alone, aware of all the sensations in your body. Imagine that you feel fatigue but just allow that fatigue until it passes, or that you notice an itch on your arm but give it no special attention, and it too passes. Or imagine that you are sitting in a poor posture and begin to feel some pain in your back. In that case you might make a minute adjustment to your sitting position and thus let your back return to normal. This is how it is in Sat Nam Rasayan. Through a process of allowing your sensations (as you allowed the itch or the fatigue), or through small appropriate adjustments (as in the small shift in your posture) you will treat the client. The only differences are that in Sat Nam Rasayan there are two bodies and one meditative mind and that the adjustments can be purely nonphysical adjustments made in consciousness. These may seem like extraordinary things and in a way they are. But they are also as natural as feeling the beat of your heart or of turning this page when you reach the bottom. Initially it will seem improbable that your meditative mind can extend to experience the consciousness in another or that it can choose to modify an event, but you will soon have a full experience of that. You have already begun the sensitive process, becoming aware of the sensations in your body and allowing them equally. And, just as allowing your fatigue might lead to its passing, allowing sensations that arise in you when you are in relation to a client leads to the completion or release of the tendencies in your client that produced those sensations.

HEALING
WITH YOUR
PRESENCE

S AT NAM RASAYAN is the way to heal with your presence. It is very subtle and yet very simple. It is easy to learn how to heal with Sat Nam Rasayan. It is actually the easiest thing imaginable because, as you are already seeing, there is nothing to do, nothing to accomplish.

In other ways of healing there may be a great deal to learn. If you want to learn to heal with acupuncture there are hundreds of points, each one connected with its related organ, and you must know how to place the needle just right, and how to diagnose, and how much of this or that you need to do in order to produce the effect that you want. It is a wonderful way to heal, and I admire those who have the intelligence and perseverance to master acupuncture. It is very effective and can bring about surprising cures. But it is hard to learn. Eventually you can become very intuitive with acupuncture and go past the rational mind in your healing work. But this will take many years and many patients.

Some ways of healing rely heavily on learned facts and on the intelligence and knowledge of the healer. A well-trained physician can instantly call to mind many possible causes of a particular symptom and will know how one drug might interact with dozens of others. At least as important, the physician will know how to access vast storehouses of information so she can intelligently research anything she is unsure of. The wise physician will also be part of a community of healers and will know which of the other members of the community might be better able to serve the patient when the physician's own knowledge or experience is inadequate.

Other healing ways are more intuitive. Psychotherapists and massage therapists are somewhat less dependent on the healer's familiarity with a body of knowledge and are more dependent on an ability to empathize with patients or sense their needs. These healers need a certain clarity of intuition, more so perhaps than their allopathic brothers and sisters, and their work depends more on accumulated wisdom than on accumulated knowledge.

Some other forms of healing are still more empathic or intuitive. Shamanistic healing is almost totally dependent on a healer's ability to alter his state of consciousness. He may "know" few facts but have an intimate knowledge of a particular transcendent world where he has access to powers and knowledge not normally available. By entering into that other world on behalf of his patient he can return with the means to effect a cure.

These different healing ways are positioned along a continuum, a spectrum ranging from the most knowledge-based to the most consciousness-based methods. Each has its place, its special value, and a culture or subculture in which it is most at home. But all these ways have something in common. They all require a skill, something that only the very practiced can do. If you are to be a good physician you must be very intelligent and very diligent as well as sympathetic and caring. If you wish to master acupuncture you must acquire a great deal of knowledge and develop your intuition as well.

Healing with Your Presence

As a shaman you will need a special gift as well as years of training. In a word, in each of these ways you will need to be good at something. You will need to know your field. You will need to know how to manipulate your tools, whether they are drugs or needles or psychic powers. In each case you must engage the client or patient as an other that needs your help, as someone with a problem that you are going to help solve. In each case you will exert a force so as to create change.

There is nothing wrong with any of this. These are all valid and valuable ways of healing. But Sat Nam Rasayan is different. In Sat Nam Rasayan we are able to heal, not because we apply a force to our clients but simply because we relate to them in a particular, conscious way. We relate to them, or to their difficulties, in a sensitive way, with awareness. We relate to them and then feel the sensations of our own experience. We allow those sensations to be as they are, and we find that those sensations change, and as they do, healing happens. It is not, as in all the other methods, that we bring about a cure or even that we facilitate healing. It is only that we access a space in which healing happens. We don't do it at all. It happens and we witness it. The marvelous thing is that in this method we are freed from the responsibility of being smart or clear or empowered. We only have to be aware and hold the intention that healing will occur. We don't have to be good or spiritual or even in a particularly good mood. We need only be kind and aware, and that can happen now.

In Sat Nam Rasayan the healing process can begin almost immediately. It only requires that you let go of some other ideas and concepts of what a healer is. If you can read these few words with an open mind and then practice, not according to your beliefs about healing but according to this simple method, you will engage in the essence of healing. And, if you are a physician or a shaman or heal with herbs, you will be able to do that work in a new way.

⚔ Heal with Your Presence

Sit now for some more practice. It is time to begin working with another, so enlist a partner, someone who is willing to lie down and relax while you act as healer. Tune in and then begin as a fool would begin, admitting that you know nothing, and let's see where that might lead. You have only your sensations and nothing else to guide you: no beliefs, no knowledge, and no desires or fears. It doesn't matter where your sensations seem to arise from: your perceptions, your emotions, or somewhere else. Just allow the sensations to be there, as they are, in this moment. This is all you need to work with. Be humble, acknowledging that your awareness might still be primitive. Be willing to practice just feeling. Sit silently and listen and feel and recognize that you don't know anything, that you have no techniques, that you have never done this exact thing before, that this moment and all that it might bring to you is totally new.

Be an ordinary person, not an expert. Let go of trying to be more pure or more spiritual or insightful. Just accept the way you feel, the way you are. You will feel sensations that you are not comfortable with—you must allow these. Don't try to get rid of imperfections or they will become like enemies to you. Don't try to focus on the breath or on a mantra, using it to improve yourself, but allow the breath to be as it is, and if a mantra is present in your mind, allow it to be there and simply feel what it is like to be in its presence.

Allow all your sensations and then begin to equalize your awareness of them. Recognize that they are all happening at once.

Healing with Your Presence

Do not fixate on any one of them. Drop the struggle to sort out the good from the bad. Transcend good and bad altogether. Transcend hope and fear, pleasure and pain, and let your attitude be very simple. This is a natural process—just be with the material that this moment has brought to you.

Once you feel stable in your equalized awareness, aware of all your sensations but concentrating on none of them, touch your partner lightly on the arm. Don't worry about technique. The simpler the better. Notice, as you touch your partner, that you feel new sensations, ones that arise in relation to him or her, but do not focus on these either. Just allow them. If you try to understand them or categorize them, you will be feeding them energy. Be aware of their presence in you, allow them, and equalize your awareness of them, recognizing that they too are happening in this moment, simultaneously with all your other sensations. Perceive yourself, in this time and place, just as you are. It is not that you are feeling your partner, only that you feel whatever is in you. Allow. Resist the temptation to try to understand your partner.

Allow whatever appears. Allow your speeding mind, or your feeling of fatigue. Allow your restlessness or anger or discomfort. No matter what may appear, allow it equally with all the other experience of this moment. Above all, do not concentrate on anything, no matter how intense it might be. Continue in this way for a few minutes more or until you have a feeling of completeness. Perhaps you have felt some sensations that were quite intense compared to others but then, after a while, they were less so. That might be a good time to end this treatment, but don't strive for that particular experience. If it occurs, fine; if not, that is also fine. When you are done with this or any of the other practice sessions, make note of how you and your partner feel, what the effect of your healing seems to be. You don't want to look for some particular effect but just objectively recognize whatever has happened.

*What you are doing with Sat Nam Rasayan is researching con-
sciousness and applying consciousness as a healing act. With this exercise you have begun your actual practice of healing. I suggest that
you not worry too much just now about the effects of what you are
doing. But do practice with the sensitive process as much as you are
able. To summarize the sensitive process up to this point: you first
tune in and open the sensitive space by allowing all of your sensations. Next you equalize, by recognizing that all sensations are happening in this moment and by letting go of any concentration. Then
you touch your partner and allow all the new sensations, along with
all the sensations that have already appeared, and equalize again to
stabilize yourself in the sensitive space.*

TOUCHING

You are not alone. In your work there is always another, a
client, a patient. Witness yourself in relation to her, feeling
whatever there is to be felt in the moments you share. She is
the "event" and you only experience the event in your sensations, in yourself. This event is nothing you could have prepared for, nothing you could have expected. Each client is the
most rare of events, utterly singular, utterly unique, unlike
any event you have ever experienced or will ever experience
again. No compass can orient you to the landscape of this
event; only your intent to heal can guide you here.

You know nothing of your client, your event, only of her
effect on you. That is all you can ever really know of anything,
and all you can work with, so this knowledge, these sensations, are most precious. Each sensation, and there are a
seemingly infinite number of them, is equally precious. You
are filled with endless waves of sensation, and sensations between these sensations. Relating to your event, this client, is

like plunging into an endless ocean of experience, an ocean
of a million waves of experience, a billion ripples of reality, a
trillion shimmering droplets of sensation, an infinity of
ocean, wave after wave breaking on the shore of your awareness, an unending phantasm of sensations, holding you in its
trance.

Approach such an event with care, lest the perfection of it
be disturbed by your ideas. Ask your client to lie on a comfortable mat and sit yourself at her side. Sit close, but not
quite touching, and take what time you might need to prepare yourself, to enter the sensitive space, this space of endless sensation and pure experience. Touch her lightly on her
arm and she becomes your event, and now you will be privileged to know yourself in relation to her. Sitting close, you
won't have to lean and can be comfortable.

There is no meaning in this gesture of touching her arm
but still it is important to get it just right. You are not trying
to give her something with this touch, not trying to communicate feelings or concern, nor trying to gain anything. You
only want to be in a relation with her, and this simple gesture
tells you both that you are. The relation could be established
other ways, you could hold her hand or gaze at her from
across the room, but this touching of her arm seems natural
and not too magical, not as if you are about to perform some
miracle, healing her at a distance. It is a normal, neutral act.
She expects something like this and might be startled by
something more or less.

When you touch her, this client becomes your event, she
with whom you are choosing to work at this time. You want
the touch to be just right, neutral, empty of meaning, something she can relax with. Your touch is respectful of the sensations you are about to experience, and so it is nothing in

itself. Hold her arm as you might hold a small bird. Ask for nothing with this holding. It is just a fragment of a larger process that establishes your place in a field of sensitivity. It is a bit of how you relate to this event.

This touch is a small, unimportant part of the whole process, but I find that I love it nevertheless. It is a beginning and I treasure it. Use this touch as a tool, a beginner's tool. It is how you individualize the client as your event. Later you may not need it; you may simply open the space, although you may continue to use touch out of habit, or for appearance' sake. The sensitive process is a vehicle, a way to arrive at the Sacred Space of Sat Nam Rasayan where healing happens. This touch is a part of that, nothing more, nothing less, just a touch.

KNOWING

How do we come to know something? By what process do you know that you like being with a certain friend or that it is cold outside? There is really only one way. Everything is known through your senses. Certainly you know the taste or feel of a dish of pasta in this sensitive way. Or, when someone calls you, the phone rings and there is a particular sensation that you experience. Your rational mind might tell you that you are hearing the ring with your ears but that is only partly the case, and it is definitely not what your experience of the ring is. If you were asleep when the phone rang you would have one experience. If you had been waiting for news about a seriously ill relative you would have another experience. If you were either startled by the ring or were far from the phone and hardly heard it, these would produce different experiences. But in any case, the experience would not necessarily be in your ears. It would be experienced as a set of sensations somewhere in your body. It is these sensations, these feelings, that you know, and nothing else.

It may take a little research into your own experience before you can agree with this. Imagine yourself in each of these different situations. What would it be like if you were right next to the phone or far away when it rang, if you were expecting a call from a loved one or news about someone who was very sick? In each case the ring would be experienced differently, and if you pay close attention you will see that the different experiences are different in that they result in different sensations *in your body*.

Our entire universe, the universe that we actually experience, is a feeling universe. What we know is what we feel. We experience our feelings and they alone are known by us. Everything else is based on that knowledge. The conclusions of the rational mind, those of the intuitive mind, the assumptions about what might happen next, emotional reactions to an event—all of these things are not known but are derived from what is known: our sensations, our actual experience. If you whisper that you love me, I will feel sensations, and it is not easily predictable what these sensations might be. I am speaking of the initial sensations that could include a flutter behind my left kneecap and a peculiar tightening in the space between my shoulder blades. These sensations are what I can know. I may then react to these sensations. I may draw some conclusions about your state of mind or have thoughts about our relationship's future. It could be that my thoughts would lead to other sensations, such as a warm feeling in the region of my heart or a tightening in the pit of my stomach. These latter sensations are also "known," in the sense that we are using that word, but as for your state of mind—I cannot directly know that, I can only infer it from my sensations.

This may or may not be a handicap in everyday life. If you are quite neutral, the conclusions you draw may be well founded. Your intuition will be accurate. Your actions, based on these conclusions, will be appropriate. But if you are in an emotional frame of mind, either positive or negative, your emotions will color your conclusions and then your words or actions may create undesirable effects. Meditation's primary purpose is the development of a neutral mind, one which is open to experience as it is, a mind that does not color experience with the dye of ego or self-preservation.

In our healing practice we aim for absolute neutrality and stability in the healing space. That means that no matter what our experience, no matter how pleasant or unpleasant our sensations may be, we will not concentrate attention on any one sensation or group of sensations. In other words, no matter what we feel, we will remain neutral and just feel. This is what Richard had to do to heal himself, and this is the sensitive space we have been discussing—the space in which all is allowed equally and we simply recognize what we feel. With time and practice using the sensitive process, you may also feel a moment of transcendence, a moment when you know more than sensations. This is when one enters the Sacred Space, when one comes to also know the consciousness in the event one relates to.

Of course, I can also "know" that six plus eleven equals seventeen or that this device in front of me is a computer and that it is 1:16 P.M. I know my name, I know where I am, and I know how to sew on a button. I know what I did yesterday and I think I know some of what I will do tomorrow. But, of the world around me, as it is occurring in this moment, I can only know directly what I feel. Anything else is secondarily known, recalled from memory, or predicted, but not directly known.

Upon careful examination, you will see that other sorts of knowing are also based on sensation. If your name is Alyce and someone calls you Martha you will experience certain sensations. They will be different from the ones you would have had if the person had gotten your name right. That is a part of how you recognize one statement as true and one as false. You know your sensations in relation to the "event" of the false statement. But you do not know anything about the individual's intent or how he or she is feeling. Any conclusions you may draw are based on emotion, prior experience, or logical inference, but they are certainly not based on a direct experience of the other's inner state.

Continue to research this. What do you actually know at this moment? How do you know that you are sitting down or riding on a subway? Is knowing your age a different sort of knowledge? In Sat Nam Rasayan we don't care so much that you know your age or your client's name. But we care very much that you know your sensations. It is upon this direct knowledge that the sensitive process is based.

In the way we are using the word, "knowing" has a very precise meaning. In everyday speech we may use the word differently but here we use it only to refer to what it is that we can be absolutely sure of in this fraction of a second. When the word is used in that way, you will see that you can only know what you feel. We will be quite dogmatic about this. In fact, the First Dogma of Sat Nam Rasayan is

Regarding any event, all you know is what you feel.

FEELING

Another thing to understand, another precise concept that will help you to open the sensitive space of Sat Nam Rasayan and ultimately help you to live your life, is that you cannot feel your client (your "event"), you can only feel yourself in relation with the other. This is very important. If you don't understand this, it will lead to a lot of confusion. In the beginning a student may say that he feels "a problem with my client's heart" or that the client "is tense in the lower part of her spine." But how could the student know such a thing? You might think that it is possible to know about another but if you examine this idea closely you will see that this is not the case. When a mother puts her lips on her baby's forehead and says that the baby has a fever, what she is really saying is that she concludes that the baby has a fever because her lips felt warm when she touched them against her baby's forehead. What she knows is the warmth in her lips, not the baby's fever.

As I write these words, I am sitting by a bay on a hazy morning. In the distance, on the other side of the little island we have camped on, I hear a loon's cry. To the east a still lukewarm sun just begins to burn through the fog. A light breeze comes up and I begin to look forward to a day of sailing. All that I see and hear in my surroundings I first experience as sensations. I feel the breeze on my skin and then think of my boat. I know the sun not as a ball of fire 93 million miles away but as warmth on my face, a faint and not unpleasant ache in my brow, and a vague flutter deep in the right side of my chest. When the loon cries I know it first as a certain lifting feeling all through my left side. These feelings are my experience. "Sun" and "loon" and "breeze" are names given to my experience, conceptions of it nowhere near as rich as the experience itself. The feelings are what I know; everything else is interpretation, or reaction, or naming of my experience. When I stay with my feelings and let go of the interpretations, names, and reactions, my experience is much more intense. By simply being present I know this moment in my sensations, and mine is the quiet joy of being in the presence of the infinite. This is the way I choose to live.

The same is true with any relationship. A student of Sat Nam Rasayan might feel something that he interprets as meaning that the client has a heart problem, but it is the feeling and not the interpretation that is important at this stage. If he is very experienced his interpretation might be quite right, but in the beginning it is best not to look for or rely on interpretations of sensations. For now, just feel what you feel, recognize it as your feeling, and let it go at that.

Can you feel fire? Can you feel the earth? No. What you feel is heat, or the pulling of gravity against your frame. You cannot even see this page. What you can feel in relation to this page is the way that the light reflected off it affects you. When you understand this distinction it will, on the one hand, free you from the onerous task of trying to know what you don't know and, on the other hand, give you back the joy of knowing what you *can* know: your own experience.

It is true that you will eventually develop skill at diagnosis if you keep working with Sat Nam Rasayan. This is not at all surprising, nor does it contradict what I have just said. Actually, you already "diagnose" in everyday life. The mother, based on her feelings, accurately diagnosed her baby's fever. If your friend's face looks downcast and her posture is slouched, your feelings in relation to her may tell you, based on your experience, that she is sad. You are very experienced, because you have lived in the company of many people with many different moods, and without hesitation you can make your diagnosis of sadness. But for our purposes it is important to recognize that you do not know she is sad, you only can know how you feel in relation to her. It is only your experience that tells you she is probably sad. In everyday life this is good enough, but it is inadequate in Sat Nam Rasayan, and it is inadequate if we hope to know peace and joy in each moment. In our healing work, we are not gathering data, so there is never a time when we can say that we have gathered enough data and therefore can draw a conclusion. We are avoiding the trap of thinking that we *know*, when we are, in fact, only surmising.

In most other forms of healing, diagnosis is based on experience plus the interpretation of data. But in Sat Nam Rasayan we can't do this. If we do, if we insist that we know what is happening in the client, we will, at the moment we draw our conclusion, tend to become less aware and less sensitive to additional feelings. In a similar way, in the moment that I labeled that piercing cry "loon," I experienced the sound less fully and I lost some of the ecstasy of pure experience. In Sat Nam Rasayan awareness is everything. Allowing whatever new sensations may appear in the relation is all-important. This must continue as long as we are in the relation.

Recognize that you do not know the event (your client, or his or her problem). What you know is what you feel in relation to the event, and that is all. Thus we have another rule. In learning to work in the sensitive space, the Second Dogma of Sat Nam Rasayan is

You do not experience an event,
you feel your sensations in relation *with it.*

62

INCLUDING

Since all-inclusive awareness lies at the heart of Sat Nam Rasayan, as well as at the heart of a joyful life, we need to ask, "What do we actually include?" Imagine yourself in a relation with your client, sensitively aware of all the feelings in yourself, when suddenly your recently injured knee starts to hurt or you think of your deceased mother and feel a heaviness in your heart. What do you do with these feelings? They might seem to be irrelevant distractions from the task at hand, something to be ignored so that you can be fully aware of the sensations in relation to your client. But consider the implications of such a conclusion. If you deem the pain in your knee irrelevant, it will have to be set aside, somehow pushed out of your awareness. How can you do that? How can you not feel? Some boundary will have to be erected, a sort of wall down the middle of your awareness with "relevant" feelings on one side and "irrelevant" feelings on the other. Or you might try to suppress the feeling, tucking it away, out of sight. Then you will not have a wall but more of a box, a place to hide the unwanted.

The problem with these strategies is that there is no end to them. If the knee pain is not relevant, what about the feeling of air moving across the skin of your hand? Is that to be included or not? What about the flutter of a muscle contracting between your ribs, or the tightening of your stomach? Which sensations are included and which are not? How can you ever know, how could you make such a judgment? How can you stand back and witness your sensations, choosing to include some and exclude others?

Even if you were able to make such distinctions, what would be the cost? What would you have to do to exclude some sensations and include others? It takes a good deal of energy and powerful defenses to maintain such boxes and boundaries, so we simply don't try. In Sat Nam Rasayan we say that we cannot discriminate against anything that appears in the relation. If an airplane passes overhead while you are in a relation with someone, the airplane (or more precisely the sensations that arise in you in relation to the sound of the airplane) is completely included. If you have had a headache for three days before your client arrives for her treatment you cannot say, "The headache has nothing to do with this client." If it appears in the relation it is included. No sensation is segregated, just as none is favored. If there is a thought, there are the sensations of having had that thought and those sensations are included also.

Isn't this also the way to live? As the sun burns off the morning haze and the breeze freshens, my daughter begins to noisily crash around our campsite. Are those sounds a disturbance? Do I ask her to be quiet so that I can enjoy the morning? Or do I include her sounds in my experience? What about these mosquitoes? I may brush them away, preferring not to be bitten, but I am peaceful only as long as my daughter's racket and the mosquitoes' buzz are allowed their rightful places in my consciousness. Insofar as I fight the presence of these things or try to exclude them I will experience something other than peace—frustration perhaps, or even anger. Our habit is to try to exclude the undesirable and to seek out more of the pleasant. This might at first seem reasonable enough in everyday affairs but it is limiting nevertheless. As we do this we shut down a part of ourselves and know less of the richness of life.

In Sat Nam Rasayan, as in the rest of life, our attitude can be inclusive. We can approach our client, our event, totally free of all judgment, totally willing to be present with whatever is placed before us. Thus, the Third Dogma of Sat Nam Rasayan is

Everything which appears in the relation
is included in the relation.

INTENTION

So far these dogmas are logical enough. They may represent new ways of thinking about our experience, but they do make sense and should be easy enough to accept. The next element is a little different. Now we need to recognize something that is further outside of our everyday experience, although it will soon seem clear enough.

When you are stable in the Sacred Space or the sensitive space of Sat Nam Rasayan, when, that is, you allow all your sensations and concentrate on none of them, any intention that occurs in your consciousness will affect your event. In Sat Nam Rasayan we always have the intention to heal That is basic and unchanging. We always hold that intention and because we do, a healing effect occurs in the client. There may be additional, subsidiary intentions, such as an intention for the enhancement of the immune system or for the release of tension. If, having become stable in your space, you introduce the intention that your client will relax, there will be a relaxing effect in the client as a consequence of that intention. Having such intentions in our own consciousness affects our clients.

Why is this so? Why is it that mere intention can have an effect on your event? Remember that we are not doing any sort of energy work or directing a force of some kind. In fact, we are not using any tools at all. It is not like having the intention of driving in a nail, which we realize through the action of picking up a hammer and striking the nail on its head. Other healing methods are more like the hammer and nail whereby the intention is translated into an action. The action could be as subtle as the movement of psychic energy or as physical as a chiropractor's adjustment. But in Sat Nam Rasayan we are working only with consciousness, and you might well ask: how does consciousness create an effect?

The answer lies in the nature of the particular consciousness of Sat Nam Rasayan. When we enter the healing space our consciousness escapes from its usual prison. Our point of view drops away along with the false sense of having a center around which all else revolves. We then experience existence without the usual false barriers between self and other. Without boundaries, consciousness is wherever it chooses to be. Without boundaries, consciousness affects whatever it is in relation to. Without boundaries, consciousness penetrates whatever it is individualized to.

In Sat Nam Rasayan there is no egocentric point of view, no sense of the healer *here* working on the client *there*. You even step beyond the sense of a "you" who feels sensations. The sensations are important but you recognize that they are taking place in the middle of nowhere, in space. It is as if all the sensations that arise are occurring not in you, but in a space. As a healer you are developing your relation to that space. In the space you are one with the sensations. There is no suppression of feeling, nor do you get carried away by your feelings. The way we work with sensations is to allow them, to relate to their basic quality, their pure "is-ness," without polluting our sensations with concepts about them. We do this successfully only when the sense of "I" is out of the picture, and we can relinquish our personal point of view.

This point of view might have different qualities at different times. Sometimes it is the sense of spatial distance—I am here and you are there. At other times the point of view is more of a visualization of what the other looks like through our eyes. And sometimes it is even more subtle: the sense of a difference or a distinction between you and your event. In our work we are not trying to "deal" with the sensations, to resolve them or to process them in some way. Rather we only want to know them as they are, without any resistance to the experience of them and without magnifying them. To do this we let go of the point of view. When we succeed at this simple task something marvelous happens; the confusion of thoughts and emotions and feelings *about* our sensations is transmuted into a direct knowledge *of* our sensations. The consequence is profound. Without a point of view there is no separation, no distinction, between the event and the consciousness of the event. Your consciousness and the consciousness in the event merge. Each affects the other. Without the point of view there is no reason that you cannot modify your event as easily as you might modify your own individual consciousness.

If you were in a peaceful, meditative space and introduced the intention that you would release still more tension or that you would become more aware of your mate's need for affection, your intention would affect you, manifesting in your body as relaxation or in your awareness as sensitivity to your partner's needs. The intentional "movements" made in your consciousness would lead to specific effects. In the same way, in Sat Nam Rasayan the intention to heal leads to an effect in your event. Letting go of your point of view allows this. It leads to the immersion of consciousness in experience, or the elimination of the distinction or distance between event and healer, and this in turn creates the space in which consciousness can modify existence. The Fourth Dogma of Sat Nam Rasayan, the one that requires a step outside the confines of our usual view of reality, is

Any intention you put into the relation
will affect the relation in some way.

These thoughts are the foundation of our work in Sat Nam Rasayan. The sensitive space, which these dogmas help to define, is our way of working in the beginning. It is a process designed to bring us to a transcendent consciousness in which our intent can affect another. It is the vehicle we use to proclaim that any condition that occurs in our experience is workable, that nothing need be rejected. The same principles apply to living a peaceful life. To arrive at our goal of healing we allow whatever happens to our state of mind or body, while holding to our intention to heal.

BEYOND DOGMA

Before going on there is one more dogma that you need to know about. It will later become the most important dogma of all. The Fifth Dogma of Sat Nam Rasayan is

There is no dogma.

You see, most everything that we have spoken of up to this point, and a good deal of what follows, is nothing more than a method, a process, that we use to direct ourselves toward a particular state of consciousness known as the Sacred Space. Once that Space is known, through practice within the lineage of Sat Nam Rasayan, the way that we have gotten there will prove to be an encumbrance—just another concept standing in the way of still deeper knowledge. The process will have to be left behind just as one leaves a boat on the shore after using it to cross a river. Further progress would surely be limited if the once useful boat were to be hefted onto our shoulders and carried along as we continued on our journey. We eventually will need to leave behind all the dogmas (including the fifth!) after they have carried us as far as they are able. Once on the yonder shore, once we have entered the Sacred Space, our concepts can't help us, and their further use will only stand in the way. At the moment that we begin to have a direct, transcendent relation with the client, this system of ours no longer makes sense. We are using the sensitive process only so you can learn to have that direct relation. But this is getting ahead of ourselves. For now we need to have certain experiences, and we will use our dogmas and the sensitive process in order to have them. Later on some of what we learn will be left behind, a vehicle that no longer serves.

BEING EMPTY

Normally, in everyday consciousness, we have little opportunity to explore the Sacred Space of Sat Nam Rasayan, or any other sacred space for that matter, and so we have few opportunities to be transcendent. One reason for that is simply that we are almost constantly concentrating on one thing or another. When we concentrate, awareness decreases and we are only aware of the one object on which we concentrate. A moment later we might be concentrating on something else entirely but still we are concentrating, aware of only one thing at a time, out of all the infinite possibilities. This is an inherently unstable condition, this moving of the mind from one thing to another in an endless series of separated and distinct moments of concentration. There is little flow to it and the objects of concentration hardly relate to one another. The mind is fragmented and its power is dissipated.

Another reason that we rarely enter the Sacred Space is that our inner selves are cluttered. We are full to the top with every imaginable concept, notion, and name for our experience, so much so that we are unaware of what we are actually feeling. We are so busy classifying and naming our experience that we never really know what it is we are experiencing. You might see a person walk into your office and in a split second you evaluate that person and classify him or her by age, sex, race, economic class, intent, possible risk to you, health status, and a thousand other things. What you are doing is putting simple names or labels on complex experiences. In doing so you lose awareness of your sensations, of your actual experience. Or, while on a walk, you might stop to look into a gallery window. Inside, a beautiful sculpture gets your attention. In your mind there is a moment of wonder but almost immediately you begin to label your experience: "I like that." Or you interpret your experience: "That is a statue of a young ballerina." Or your mind goes off in another direction and pictures the statue in your home or imagines what it might cost. In your crowded consciousness there is hardly any room for the wondrous sensations of your relation to the sculpture, and your experience of the moment is limited. This consciousness, in which everything is labeled or judged or compared to past experience and almost nothing is experienced fully, in the present, is not the way to live, nor is it appropriate for healing.

In contrast, if you release your concentration and judgments and naming, your mind can become neutral and silent: a delightful state indeed. It is not the silence that is important; what is important is the experience we can have within that silence. When there is silence, we have the possibility of deeply experiencing and of relating to our event within the Sacred Space. And it is in the Sacred Space that we can modify our event. There are thousands who have silence in their minds but that does not make them healers. They are certainly happier without conditions and judgment and other mental noise, but they do not necessarily produce a transcendent consciousness. What is needed is to "de-concentrate" the mind and to erase at least some of its conditions. That is the combination that will unlock the door of healing.

When you hold yourself in the sensitive space and don't move, the relations in the space become intensified. The space itself becomes intensified. You will feel this as you practice. You stabilize your space and begin to increase your space, allowing more and more, and it feels as if you are going deeper into the relation with your client. You reduce the sense of differentiation in the relation and you and your client begin to feel very integrated. This is the beginning of a sacred relation.

Recently I treated Carla, who was in a lot of emotional pain. She had begun by telling me how idyllic her childhood had been, how much she had learned from her parents, how wonderful it was that her father had died while singing a religious hymn. This was her myth. Her voice was loud, too loud, and her animated gestures seemed forced, as if she were trying to look energized but was really quite tired. In the ten years since her father's death she had lived as far from her family as she could without actually leaving the country, and now she had returned to try to take care of her mother, who was killing herself with alcohol. When she was with her, her mother picked and scratched at her arms nervously until she bled. Among other things, Carla began to recall a child-hood memory of having to wait in the family car while her father met with his lover.

When I began to treat Carla with Sat Nam Rasayan, the first moments were smooth, just as her surface story had been. As soon as I individualized to particular aspects of her condition everything became very intense. I felt numbness in my arm and headache and other sensations that had no particular name. It was as if I were suffering her pain. I held the space stable and equalized my awareness of the sensations, not concentrating on any one of them and letting go of any ideas about my experience. I opened the space to more and more sensations, and as I did, there was a reduction of the pain I felt, even as the sense of distance between us decreased. I introduced intentions, to balance the water element (so that her emotions might flow) and to balance the earth element (so that she might feel the security of that), and as I did so there was renewed intensity (see the "Elements" chapter on page 125). Intention is a direction to the relation, a turning within the space. It is nothing really, just a movement in the mind, a quiet word to oneself. Intention is no more than a gentle current in a vast sea. But intention will intensify the relation.

Allowing all I felt and opening still further produced a new flow of energy where before there had been resistance. After a short while, I was able to make some movements (the feeling of this is like the feeling of changing one's mind) and there was a sense of completion. When Carla sat up a minute later, she was visibly changed. She was calm, her face was relaxed, and her voice was soft and peaceful. Her breath was slower and deeper and she talked of her need to be closer to her real feelings. I had not done anything to Carla. Everything I did was in and with my own awareness. I had recognized my sensations and held my awareness of them. I held it and allowed whatever appeared and made a few small movements in the space of the relation. Working in this way, through the space, reduced her pain.

To heal we need to be empty of concentration and judgment, and we need to be stable in this state. This is what our sensitive process does for us. This sensitive process was created so that we can help others to heal. Our purpose in using that space is that in it our capacity to serve is incredibly increased. The essence of our simple task is to reduce the impulse to control our experience.

Although consciousness is potentially unlimited, in everyday life it is severely limited by the limits in our own awareness and the desire to control. Just now I notice a woman walking past my house. She is exercising, walking fast. But this woman carries some tension in her hips and her chest, and it causes her to walk in a funny way, with her toes pointed out and her head down. This puts a limit on her walking. Consciousness is like that. The places where we hold our conditions, beliefs, desires, and fears are like the physical holding of tension in this woman's hips and chest, and they limit the consciousness just as her tension limits her walking.

THE
SACRED
SPACE

THE SPACES of Sat Nam Rasayan are not at all like the space inside my desk drawer, or the empty spaces on the computer screen. They are not spaces in the same way that a two- or three-dimensional enclosure is a space. A gymnasium is a space in which one might play basketball, the empty space of a chalkboard is where one might write an equation. There may also be a space in my schedule, a place defined by the dimensions of time, perhaps an hour in duration, a space in which we could get together and go for a walk. Some spaces are defined by both space and time—we will meet for an hour at my office or I will kayak for a month along the coast of Maine.

But there are also spaces in consciousness; a skillful counselor will set aside all of her other concerns while her client is with her. During their time together her focus is on her client. An artist may lose, for a time, all awareness of anything other than his painting, or a lover may totally focus on her beloved, with nothing else in that particular space of consciousness. This sort of space is defined not by time or space but by attention.

We exist in spaces with specific boundaries of awareness and these boundaries are constantly changing. No matter if we are locked in solitary confinement, or are hang gliding high above a gorgeous, boundless landscape, the shape of the space of our awareness is determined by what we do in our consciousness. The thrilling part of this is that *we always have the ability to choose all the dimensions of our space.*

As an example of how one might purposefully create a space in consciousness, consider my writing space, the one I am in right now. I have a good sense of the best space for writing. It is a *physical place* (my office, this chair, in front of this computer); it is a *time* when things will be reasonably quiet around the house; it is a level of *mental concentration* somewhat tempered by well-timed flights of fancy but essentially limited to the topic at hand. Most significantly, I know how to create or open this space. I have learned through trial and error how to enter the space and how to remain stable in it, and I am good at this process. I don't, for example, yield to every impulse to call a friend, but I do occasionally get up and make a cup of tea. I have learned to maintain a very particular space, for a very particular purpose, and when I have done so, writing happens. It is not that I write but rather that I enter a space in which writing happens.

So it is with the sensitive space or with the Sacred Space of Sat Nam Rasayan. These are not themselves healing but are the spaces in which healing happens. Just as my writing space creates the conditions in which writing happens, the spaces of Sat Nam Rasayan are a deliberate creation of the conditions favorable to our healing intent.

While it is relatively simple to describe spaces that have physical dimensions and exist in past, present, or future time, it is a more daunting task to describe the dimensions of sacred spaces. They have some dimensions that we can speak of, but we will find that in regard to many of their dimensions we can speak only of what the spaces are not. In writing about the Sacred Space of Sat Nam Rasayan, the best I can do is point you in the right direction like an archer taking aim at a target that stands hidden behind an opaque veil. I can send the arrow in the right direction but the arrow must leave the bow, arch through the gap between archer and target, and pierce the veil on its own. You will never "know" the target until you reach it. There is simply no way to improve on this, there is no way for the arrow of your consciousness to know the target without experiencing it for itself. As we proceed from here in this ultimately unavailing attempt to define the Sacred Space of Sat Nam Rasayan, we will necessarily say a good deal more of what the space is not, than of what it is. In this way we will use our limited language to try to point beyond language. We will aim our arrow at a target that is hidden on the thither side of an eschatological veil, a target that will remain forever indescribable.

Fortunately, our object is healing, not talking, and so this difficulty with language is ultimately trivial. Language is always symbolic, it always deals in concepts. A poet uses language to point to a concrete experience beyond words. We need to do the same thing. We seek an experience beyond form and will use language and our senses to reach beyond language and sense into a Space where reality and experience are one. This Sacred Space will be discovered to be a space of transcendence, a place without any of the *interpretations* of reality that our rational minds usually confuse with the experience of reality itself.

This Sacred Space of ours is always there and it always has been. It has its own existence. The ability to access the Sacred Space is preserved in the lineage that holds it intact. The Space is an emanation of God, a fountain of healing miracles, a Space in which all our rules are broken except the rule of intention. In this magical Space intention creates effect. The Sacred Space is the particular way that God manifests in one who practices Sat Nam Rasayan.

One of the few concrete statements that can be made about the Sacred Space is that one of its parameters is the intent to heal. But immediately upon making this statement it is necessary to recall what healing is and what it is not. Healing is not a change that takes place in a body or mind as a result of the application of an outside force. That is what we have called curing, or attempting to cure. Perhaps the most accurate synonyms for healing as we use the word are "peace" and "balance," and our intent is to help to restore these states. In doing that we might see that the body and mind are enabled to rid themselves of disease.

The balance experienced by one who is physically deteriorating and is at the threshold of death will be very different from the balance of one who has serious but not life-threatening injuries or one who is distraught over the loss of a loved one. In all cases balance might include "coming to peace," but this will have different implications for the different people involved. Balance for the injured patient might include an appropriate will to fight back against the effects of the injuries and their psychological implications, but balance for the dying patient might be primarily a matter of facing and finally letting go of fears. The one who has suffered a loss will find balance in a different way, as he or she allows grief to run its natural course, unfettered by cultural and familial demands that the process be gotten over with quickly. In all cases, though, healing is the release of conditions that hold the patient in harmful patterns or tendencies.

The healing spaces of Sat Nam Rasayan do not include the

application of force. There is no surgeon's knife, no chiropractor's adjustment, none of the chemical energy of an herb or a drug. Nor is there control of energy or an attempt to bring the being of the client into alignment with the will of God. The Sacred Space is a space of no effort, no will, and no desire of any kind. It is a space of knowing what is, as it is, at this moment, with the intent (not the desire, but the simple intent) for healing. But this intent is all important and we need to constantly maintain it when we are practicing Sat Nam Rasayan.

The Sacred Space is characterized, or bounded, by simultaneous and equal awareness of all sensations that appear. The Sacred Space is not a space that is limited by concentration. This is possibly the most central of all the defining characteristics of this space. No one experience or sensation is held in awareness to the exclusion of other experiences or sensations. Every sensation is given the same amount of attention and we are equally and fully aware of each sensation, regardless of how intense or faint that sensation might be. Everything is included and everything is allowed, equally. And, slipping immediately back into what the Space is not, it is not a space of discrimination, judgment, or preference for one sensation over another.

Still another parameter of the Sacred Space is that in it there is no point of view. Again we speak of what the space is not. In normal consciousness we maintain a point of view. *I* have this experience. *I* look at that. *That* sound is coming from *there*. Always there is the belief that *I* stand at the center of my experience and all the events I am in relation to are located peripherally. Even a sensation of an itch on my forehead is somehow separated and apart from the one who feels the itch. We live in a universe dominated by subject and object. *I* am here, *you* are there, and *they* are in the next room. I exist within narrowly imagined boundaries, with the rest of the cosmos outside of them.

We humans, although a part of the whole that we call the universe, perceive ourselves as separated from all else by barriers of time and space. We think of ourselves as individuals, somehow apart from the rest, and this illusory separateness tends to limit us to caring for our personal desires, seeking after our own preferences, and avoiding that which we fear or dislike. We limit ourselves to a few situations that please us and a few individuals we are comfortable with. Our spiritual task is to break free of these self-imposed restrictions and to be willing to embrace the whole of our experience: to break down the subject-object barrier, to break through the illusory divisions we impose upon the universe, and to recognize that subject and object are one.

These boundaries of the individual self are essentially experienced as a sense of distance between the observer and the rest of reality. The itch on my forehead is felt to be *there*, as opposed to *here*, where my consciousness seems to be. The fact is, however, that it is the forehead that experiences the itch, not "me," and there is no distance whatsoever between event and experience. And if I gaze out into the night sky and marvel at the billions of stars arrayed there, the experience of those points of light supposedly millions of light years distant is not there on the far reaches of the universe, but here in the flutter of feeling in my chest and in the quickening of my breath.

Entrance into the Sacred Space of Sat Nam Rasayan requires letting go of our belief in ourselves as subjects separate from the objects of our experience. Our brain functions to ensure our survival; that is its job, the imperative handed

80

The Sacred Space

down through ages of evolution. To do its job it receives, stores, and manipulates information in such a way that consciousness is shaped into a sense of self continuously concerned with its own survival. This happens so seamlessly that we never even suspect the possibility of transcending that consciousness. But transcendence is precisely what the essence of healing requires. In the Sacred Space there is no room for separation, for point of view.

In the everyday mind the sense of self would have us believe that one who is aware is separate from the sensations that one is aware of. In Sat Nam Rasayan awareness and sensation, reality and the experience of it, are one. This leads to the breakdown of the illusion of distance, of "space" in the way that word is traditionally used. If I am here and the star I look upon is there, then there is a sense of space between the two. But if I am here and my sensation in relation to the star is also here, within this consciousness, then space or distance has seemed to disappear. In the same way, the sensation of the itch on my forehead and the perception of it also occur in the same place.

If you hear a sound, the awareness of that sound is in your body, experienced as sensation. It is easiest to see this if you can remember a time when you were startled by a loud noise. The actual experience of that was a "shock" of feelings that went through your body. It was not, "Oh, a door just slammed behind me." That was an interpretation of the shock, *from your point of view*, and that interpretation took place a split second after the shock itself. The actual experience was the shock.

It is a bit harder to recognize, but no less true, that all sound is experienced that way. To research this phenomenon, simply close your eyes now and quiet your mind. Wait for sounds to occur, carefully observing how they are experienced. You will notice that they are not "heard" in your ears or in your brain or at some imagined center of your consciousness, or somehow experienced in the next room or wherever they might come from; rather they are felt as sensations in your body. Further careful observation will reveal that the same is true with other senses such as sight or smell. Thus the star is known through the sensations in your body that arise when you are in relation to the star. There is no consciousness of photons of light striking your retina, nor is there any actual experience of the star "out there."

None of these experiences are happening to a consciousness that is fixed in some location, either "out there" or "in here." Consciousness has no location. It has no point of view, no place where it sits and observes the rest of the cosmos. It is everywhere. There is no distance between you and your experience. In the sensitive process of Sat Nam Rasayan we include any sensations that may arise, always expanding our consciousness to include whatever appears. Since all is included, there is no limit to the reach of consciousness. In the Sacred Space consciousness grows to be all inclusive. There is no sense of a separate you. There is just consciousness.

The next parameter or boundary of the Sacred Space is that it is a place of no names. Imagine that a door slams behind you. As we've already established, you don't know that event as a door slamming but as a shock of sensations in your body. The actual experience is indescribable. There are no words you might use that could convey to me what you experienced when the door slammed. If you say there was a shock I might think that I know what you mean, but that is only because I have memories of events in my own experience that were also called shocks. No language will give me your exact experience. The names that we give to our experience are not the experience itself. In the Sacred Space no sensation has a name; it just is.

The Sacred Space is also a place without judgment. This may be the boundary of the space that is hardest to maintain. When I feel a set of sensations in my foot that I call by the name "pain," my experience of that leads me to the almost instantaneous conclusion that this is an experience I want to avoid. When you feel a warm sensation on your skin as you sit in the sun, you may equally quickly find yourself attracted to this sensation. But as we examine either of these perfectly understandable but judgmental reactions, we will notice that they tend to take us away from the Sacred Space. Judgment leads to a rejection of a part of our experience or to a desire for more of another part. This is identical to rejecting a part of ourselves or desiring that there be more of a certain other aspect of our being. There can be no peace in such attitudes. Love for self and the peace that implies can only be based on a full appreciation and acceptance of who we are, in this moment, even if there is also an intention for continued personal evolution. In the Sacred Space there are no preferences, and none of the judgments that lead to them. In the sensitive space, if judgment and preference do occur, then we can only allow whatever sensations might appear in relation to *them*.

On the other hand, if we do not judge our experience, if we are able to remain neutral in relation to the reality we find ourselves a part of, we are liberated from the greatest cause of suffering in life: the demand that the conditions of our existence be other than what they actually are. If there is no judgment, it follows that there tends to be no effort. Allowing all sensation equally is the antithesis of trying to improve

83

things. Please understand that I do not mean to imply by this that you ought to accept everything as it is and never work to improve conditions in the world. Quite the contrary. If you are able to feel the effects of your experience, you will know exactly what needs to be done and will not hesitate to do it. Allowing your sensations and working to improve conditions are not at all mutually exclusive.

In the Sacred Space there are no distractions. Normally, when we are meditating or concentrating on something we have the concept that there is, on the one hand, the *goal* of our meditation or concentration and, on the other hand, distractions—anything that might keep us from the successful completion of the task. We find ourselves "trying to meditate" or "trying to concentrate." If we have set ourselves to continuously repeating a mantra, silently with each breath, and then notice that our mind has wandered off to thoughts about what else we need to be doing, or the argument we had with our partner, we will conceive of these other thoughts as distractions, will reject them as being irrelevant to our meditation, and then we will try again to concentrate. If a car alarm went off as we were meditating, the tendency would be for us to concentrate on it for at least a moment. We would experience it as another distraction, another interruption of our meditative process. With increased skill in meditation we will be less disturbed by these interruptions but we may still hold to the belief that they were outside of true meditation. But in the Sacred Space of Sat Nam Rasayan there are no distractions. Whatever appears is included equally, whether it be the shock of sensations in relation to a car alarm, a pain in the foot, or a pleasant feeling of opening in the region of the heart.

Perhaps by now you have seen the flaw in all that I have

written about the nature of the Sacred Space. No matter how well I may have done my job, I am still trying to define something beyond definition. The Sacred Space is a transcendent space. All that I have called its boundaries or parameters are conditions I have placed on it. While they may serve to help you take aim at the target, all these conditions must be dropped if you hope to ever have the arrow of your consciousness pierce the veil of unknowing and reach that target of transcendence. But, for now, go ahead and use these hints and the sensitive process to open and "enlarge" your inner space. Let conditions that might limit the space, conditions such as judgment or effort, simply drop away. Let your sensitive space become more and more unlimited. Practicing in this way, becoming ever more skillful at opening and being stable in the sensitive space, is a way of moving toward linking yourself to the lineage of Sat Nam Rasayan. As a side effect of your efforts you will also be learning more of how to live your life wisely.

A final point: When you have first come to recognize the Sacred Space you may find yourself going into the Sacred Space and passing right on through it and into deep meditation, but that is not Sat Nam Rasayan. This Space is for healing, not to improve your meditations. This is a *seva*, a service for others, and in this one way this undefinable Space is strictly defined.

⚔ Enlarge Your Inner Space

Pause now to practice. Put aside all these ideas about the nature of the Sacred Space. Sit straight and close your eyes. Allow all of the sensations that appear in your consciousness. Take your time and continually expand your awareness, allowing more and more. No-

tice any tendency to discriminate among your sensations, to feel that some are more appropriate or desirable or important than others. Notice any tendency to narrow your space. Release any such conditions and simply allow.

Notice any tendency to observe your sensations, to look at them from a separated point of view. Release that tendency, reducing the sense of distance between you and your sensations. If there is a noise, allow the sensations associated with that noise. If there is a thought, allow the sensations associated with the thought. Release any sense of yourself as separate from your experience. There is no distance; you and your experience are one. Reduce feelings of differentiation.

Equalize further. Recognize that all your sensations are happening at the same time. Let go of concentration on one sensation after another, and feel them as all equally occurring in this moment. Release any sense of sequence.

Accept that there is nothing for you to do in this space. There is no need for effort. Have no will, only the simple intention to be stable in your space. If you find that you have begun to concentrate, or to make an effort, or to feel separate from your experience, recognize the feelings of that and expand to allow those feelings as well.

If you are practicing with a partner, touch your partner now, and once again allow all the sensations that appear in your consciousness. Expand to allow more and more. Include whatever appears, without discrimination.

Equalize again. Again let go of any concentration. Recognize your concepts about your partner: how he or she looks, where he or she seems to be in relation to you, the sense of distance between you. Recognize any sense of differentiation in your relation with your partner. Go through each of these resistances, one at a time. Slowly reduce all of these tendencies by allowing the sensations of them until they are complete, until the sensations dissolve.

86

The Sacred Space

Continue to treat your partner for five or ten minutes more. Do nothing but remain stable.

EQUALIZING

Equalizing is a powerful part of our work in Sat Nam Rasayan. You are already using equalizing as you open and stabilize your sensitive space. You should be equalizing whenever you recognize a need to sustain your awareness in a stable manner. Remember that it is concentration that creates instability. Whenever you feel that you are concentrating, on one thing or on a series of things, you can get past that by equalizing. If you lose the equalization of your space your stability will be decreased and you will decrease the effectiveness of your treatments.

Have you ever had a fly land on your face when you were meditating, or been meditating when the phone rang? There are three ways that one might be immune to such "disturbances." The first is through concentration. If your meditation is based on focusing on a mantra or your breath or some other object of concentration, you could develop your power of concentration to the point where you might notice a disturbance but in an instant your concentration would be restored. A distraction would register for a split second but no longer. A tiny percentage of your attention might go into identifying the disturbance ("fly on my face") but your mind would immediately recognize the disturbance as unimportant and not worth any more of your attention. You would know that it would only increase the disturbance to wish the fly were not there or to brush it away. The experienced concentrator can create a situation in which there is only a single persistent thought such as the mantra, or a single object of attention such as the breath. Without losing concentration on the focus of the meditation the concentrator can quickly evaluate any new stimulus and dismiss it before it ever has a chance to seriously disturb the meditative process.

A second way to remain undisturbed in the face of distraction is through trance. If you were not consciously aware of a fly on your cheek, you would continue to meditate despite the fly's presence. As you read this book you probably are not consciously aware of the pressure of the book against your hand, or of the position of your left foot, so it should be easy to imagine the conscious mind not registering every stimulus. You can learn to be consciously aware of even less, to induce in yourself a trance state in which distractions to meditation are simply not registered by your conscious mind. In some spiritual traditions, this induction of trance is a skill that has been honed to a fine level.

But there is a third possibility: a particular spiritual state, different from concentration, different from trance, different from countless other spiritual states—the sensitive space. In this space we equalize and recognize that all of our sensations are happening at the same time and in the same space and that all sensations are of equal importance. There are no big sensations and no little ones, no valued ones and none that are avoided. Thus, there are no experiences and no sensations that we consider distractions. When we equalize in our healing or meditative space, and allow and include all sensations, we become stable in the space.

◢ EQUALIZE YOUR SPACE

Practice now, alone or with a partner, equalizing your space. Tune in and open the space in the usual way, allowing all sensations to happen. If you are with a partner, touch your partner and allow

more and more sensations, whatever might appear. Recognize that
all your sensations are happening in the same time and space.
Experience them as if they were all in a single plane, none standing
out above the others. Equalize in this way and experience the ef-
fects of this. Whenever you feel distracted, notice the sensations of
that and include them in the equalizing process. Whenever you
notice your tendency to concentrate, do the same thing: notice the
feelings that arise in relation to your concentration, allow the feel-
ings, and equalize. Continue in this way, holding your space stable
for ten or fifteen minutes, or more.

Equalizing is not a movement in your consciousness. It is
not like an intention to improve the liver function or balance
the earth element in a client. It is merely recognizing what is
happening. If the wind blows against your arm you feel sensation. If upon entering into a relation with your client you
feel a shock, this is sensation. Don't get lost in these sensations but allow them, without making anything special of
them. A sensation is just a sensation. What do you know other
than that you feel it? You know how it feels, and that is all. You
don't know what it might mean or if it is important. So we
equalize because there is no legitimate way to put some special value on any one sensation.

* * *

Sensations are all that you experience, all that you can actually know. When you hear a sound you immediately inter-
prete it and think, "There is a car starting outside," or, "My
phone is ringing." But your actual experience is not of the car
or the phone, not of the sound waves hitting your ears, not
even of your brain interpreting the nerve impulses that come
to it from your ears. Rather your actual initial experience is
of a slight "shock" as the sound goes through your body. We

can also call these sensations "contractions." You will recognize this shock or contraction when you first come into relationship with someone. It is the impact of that relation. You may also have the experience of not feeling anything, the sensation of no sensation, and you can also recognize that experience.

This sense of shock will be more obvious if, while you are meditating, a door slams just behind you. You will feel a shock of sensations even before your mind rushes to understand the sound and its meanings. Next your mind will want to know if this sound is a danger sign and what action it might call for. Then you will try to interpret the sound correctly. Is it a door slamming or, perhaps, a gunshot, or did the wind blow the door closed, or has someone come into your room? If you can't figure it out quickly enough, in the next second, you might wheel around and open your eyes. The less loud or abrupt the sound, the more familiar with it you might be. The more developed your ability to equalize, the less your shock and the less attention you would concentrate on the experience of the sound.

In a similar way anything that you enter into a relation with, whether it be a sound, or a client, or a client's heart or stomach, or an intention of your own (perhaps to heal the client's heart or stomach), will produce a shock of sensations in your body. While this might be clear enough with the example of a slamming door in the middle of a meditation, it might not be so obvious in more routine moments. It takes doing some research to know that this is true. As I let my eyes slowly scan the objects on my desk, I randomly enter into relation with some of them. As I do, in each case there is a slightly different sensation or set of sensations. When I look at a small picture of me together with my teacher, Yogi Bhajan, I feel a warm fullness in the right side of my chest; when I notice my water bottle, the "shock" is a tiny pulling in the muscles of my left upper arm. An unanswered letter is accompanied by a sensation in my chest and a tightening up near my throat.

When I bring to mind remote objects or people, I feel other sensations. Thinking of the van that I travel in, I feel an odd sense of movement in my pelvis. Maybe the next time I think of the van I'll notice some numbness in my arm. I am not saying that the van makes me feel the movement in my pelvis or that the water bottle leads to pulling in the muscles. I can only say that at the moment I let my attention individualize to the water bottle, there is a "shock," albeit a mild one, of sensations that I am aware of in my body. Nor do I try to interpret these feelings. I don't say that since the movement in my pelvis is something like the movement involved in walking, I must be thinking of traveling when I think of the van. Rather than interpreting or having any sense of cause and effect, I am simply aware of the sensations.

Equalizing is being aware of these sensations at the same time that you are aware of all the other sensations present in your body, giving each sensation, no matter how intense or mild it might be, the same amount of attention. Thus, when I am working with the sensitive process of Sat Nam Rasayan I will notice my hand and my foot equally, even if my foot is in pain and my hand feels about as neutral as a hand can feel.

⚔ EQUALIZE YOUR SENSATIONS

Sit now, once again, with stillness and dignity and with your eyes closed. Tune in and begin to feel all the sensations in your body. Recognize all your sensations, be aware of them, and allow them to happen to you. Be aware of discomfort, of the pull of gravity, of sound passing through you. Be equally aware of all of these, despite how intense or faint the sensations might be. Pay close attention and let yourself experience a finer and finer detail of sensation. Keep expanding to include more. Feel blood circulating, waves of energy in your nerves, and life force in each cell. Continue to equalize your sensations, allowing whatever appears in your consciousness to be included, always without concentration.

This is equalizing, a process of inclusiveness that allows each sensation without discrimination, without judgment, without analysis, without even naming the sensation or its source. Practice this over and over. It is an essential ingredient in the sensitive process of Sat Nam Rasayan. Simply include in your awareness whatever sensations might appear. The opposite of this would be to declare the discomfort in your leg or the fly on your face to be outside of the realm of your meditation, a distraction from the business at hand. If you did you would label some sensations "good" and others "bad." This would be like drawing a circle in the middle of your experience and trying to exclude from your awareness whatever was outside of that circle. If you have ever meditated with that attitude, you know that there is no end to it. No matter how often you repeat your mantra, you will always have some "irrelevant" thought. No matter how many times you might adjust your body's position, you will feel some discomfort somewhere, however slight. At some point you might switch from trying to be empty of thought, or more comfortable, to trying to ignore the thoughts or the unwanted sensations. This will usually lead to a short period of peace before a more fascinating thought appears or one of your sensations begins to again feel too intense to ignore.

The Sacred Space

Then there will be more effort or adjustment as you try to reject or escape the new disturbance. The process goes on indefinitely and the meditation is never all it could be.

Equalizing is the alternative to this frustrating way of "trying to meditate." No matter how much success you are having with equalizing, you can probably go further. There are ever new sensations arising in your awareness. There are the seemingly empty spaces between your sensations that hold less conspicuous sensations. As you open your awareness you will discover an elusive quality of experience so understated, so fine, that you never before discerned it. Allow and feel all of this with the same regard as the slamming door or the fly on your face, no more and no less.

There is another, related, meaning to this word "equalize." We also equalize by recognizing that all of our experiences of this moment are happening at the same time. This is logical enough but it is not the way that we conventionally witness our own experience. What is more habitual is for our minds to momentarily concentrate on one bit of experience after another. Even sitting in meditation, I might notice the itch on my eyelid, then notice my breath, then the eyelid again, then my breath and mantra at the same time, then a thought about the workshop I have planned, then back to the breath for a while, first noticing the feeling of my rib cage expanding, then the lift of my shoulders, then my belly going through its rhythmical changes. Then it's back again to the mantra, and then I notice a sound in the next room. In all this there is a strong sense of sequence, of one event followed by another.

But that is not the case. It is more precise to recognize that the breath, the itch, and the sound are all occurring in the same moment and that the sensations you experience in relation to each are all there at the same time, whether they have been recognized by your conscious mind or not. Equalizing occurs when we allow all the sensations to happen now, in this moment. It is the capacity to allow all sensations to be recognized at once. If all the sensations of this moment are happening now, as indeed they are, then the only way to allow all sensations is not to concentrate on any one of them. We normally experience sensations as if they were happening sequentially, because in any particular moment we concentrate on one to the exclusion of all others. In any moment we know only one sensation. In the next moment we focus on another sensation and then another. This creates the illusion of time or sequence and makes it impossible for us to experience the vastness of the reality of this moment.

Equalizing can be further understood in terms of space. When I am attracted to one bit of my reality, when I concentrate on one sensation to the exclusion of others, it is as if I were looking at it. It is like watching a tennis match from a seat very close to the net. I must turn my head away from one player in order to see the other player hit the ball. When I look to one player, all my experience is on her side of the court. When I look at the other player I experience her side of the court. My memory gives coherence to my experience of the game, but nevertheless I am first in one space and then another.

In meditation, if I allow myself to concentrate on a series of sensations, it is as if I were at a tennis match with innumerable players, each playing in his or her own court. Each object of my awareness remains separate and apparently in a separate space. Research this. As your mind focuses on one thing at a time see how that fragments your experience into separate spaces. The experience is of distance. This thing is here and that one is there, and I am somewhere between, ob-

The Sacred Space

serving both from a distance. Equalizing overcomes this spatial disintegration of consciousness, this sense of distance, just as it takes us out of the artificial sense of sequence or time. It helps us to integrate our experience. Carried to its full expression, equalizing allows us to transcend time and space.

⚰ REMAIN AWARE OF DISCOMFORT

Close your eyes now, tune in, and open the sensitive space. Equalize your sensations and then select from among them one sensation of moderate discomfort. Continue to allow and equalize all your sensations while remaining aware of the sensation of discomfort. After a time the sensation will begin to fade or have less intensity. The contraction will resolve itself, by itself, as you equalize, simply allowing the contraction equally with all your other sensations. Continue to treat yourself until you feel a sense of completion.

In healing situations your sensations or contractions will be in relation to the client. When you relate to another person and allow the sensations of that, the sensations will move or change. This is at the very center of Sat Nam Rasayan. Please understand the elegance of this, its simple beauty. Here is a way to affect the other, your event, by simply allowing the sensations in relation to the event, solely within your consciousness. There is no karma in this, no responsibility for making it come out right. You simply need to know and allow whatever is present and watch it as it comes to completion. There is no activity. You are simply being neutral and aware. The consequence of this is healing, but it is not you doing the healing. Rather, the healing happens in your presence. It is a most wonderful thing.

The culmination of equalizing is the disappearance of your point of view, the artificial notion that your consciousness has a center. In everyday consciousness you imagine that you exist "here," somewhere in your body or mind. Another person, or a sensation, or any other object of your perception is "there" at a point located some distance away. You perceive of the separation and imagine that you are experiencing reality from a point of view located somewhere inside you. You may have a pain in your toe and think of it as "my toe" and have the sense that you know the pain "down there" from a vantage point or point of view "up here." You have the same sense of remoteness in relation to almost anything you may be aware of, whether it be another person or even your own thoughts. In fact, the location of this supposed center of consciousness proves to be quite elusive if you set about trying to find it. We believe we have a center but we have no idea where it might be.

The center, of course, is a fantasy. In Sat Nam Rasayan what we do is to make the center disappear. We are able to graduate beyond the notion that our consciousness can't affect another, because we release all sense of a separation from that other. By equalizing we reduce the pressure of having a center by recognizing that the sensations are happening in the same moment and in the same space. We recognize that it is only the mind that creates the differentiation, the distance, and artificially divides our universe into subject and object.

NONRESISTANCE

Outside the window of my room, snow is falling. Tiny white dots move rapidly to and fro, and up and down, blown by gusty winds. I might react to this scene and say that the day feels cold to me, it makes me feel gloomy and wish that I was living in a warmer climate. On a different day there might be a different reaction, an anticipation of the joy of skiing, of an outing with my wife and daughter, of the invigoration of exercise out in the cold.

If I look at the weather with negative feelings, I am limited. I hold to certain conditions and they lead to constrictions, tension, a bad mood. I have meanings that I give to the snow and the low gray clouds. I *resist* my experience in complex ways. This resistance is a condition applied to my experience. In the relationship between me and the scene outside my window, there are conditions, and my experience is in a very real way predetermined. My conditions prevent me from having a totally new experience, the experience of this moment. I am experiencing my past, not the present arrayed before me, and there can be nothing new in that, and no insight, no delight, and ultimately, no healing. The past is dead, frozen in time and consciousness, and cannot be a source of transcendence.

If my reactions are more positive, if I saw the snow and began to eagerly anticipate the fun and exhilaration of playing in beautiful fresh powder, my mood would be different, perhaps more desirable. But in terms of resistance to this moment the problem is the same and I am still limited. Again there is a condition in my consciousness, a pattern of thought and a set of positive feelings that limit my relation to what exists in the here and now, precisely in the same way that the more negative feelings did.

Initially, when I notice the snow, there are preconditions and concentration, a way that my consciousness recognizes the snow and my relation to it and focuses in on that. This is a most important thing that we must learn to deal with if we are to facilitate healing. If we concentrate on one thing, if we limit our awareness, even for just a moment, there is no other experiencing, no other knowing, during that moment of concentration, and everything but the object of our concentration is excluded from our awareness. When our consciousness is limited in this way to only a single object, the *flow* of consciousness ceases. In such a circumstance transcendence is not possible. There can be no elevation because our consciousness is now conditional and limited by desire or avoidance.

Between the snow and me there is a relation. If I feel no resistance to any of my sensations, if I have no conditions in regard to them, then my consciousness and my perception of the relation with the snow will be clear and intensified. As my conditions resolve there is the possibility to become transcendent. Then I experience the snow as if I had never seen or even heard of snow before. If I have no conditions and no preconceptions about the snow, then I might truly know my own experience. And, if I both experience and know, then and only then, can I simply be.

In the moment of relation with the snow I may notice my resistance. If I can release that, the relation can become more complete. I can then be in an intense relation to the snow itself—I can have a direct experience of it with no conditions. It is when I release these ordinary conditions and resistances that I find the extraordinary.

⚹ EQUALIZE YOUR AWARENESS

Sit next to your partner. Close your eyes, tune in, and do nothing, just be aware of all of your sensations. Don't worry about anything else, just be aware. Equalize your awareness, letting there be no

The Sacred Space

concentration. When you are stable, enter into the space of the rela-
tion with your partner, lightly touching him or her on the arm.
Now observe your resistances, the areas where your mind tends to
concentrate itself. Some sensations may feel quite normal, others
quite extraordinary, but let all receive equal attention. Why let one
sensation be your focus? Why choose one over the others? Why is one
more interesting than the rest? The fascinating and the normal are
happening at the same time, why choose only one of them? Don't
try to find any specific sensations, or to understand or interpret
anything. Just allow life to be exactly as it is. Remember, no concen-
tration. Continue in this way for ten minutes or more.

In this practice of the sensitive process you are first aware
of everything that happens in you. Then you open the space
of the relationship with the client and become aware of
everything that happens in that relation. Some things appear
as a resistance. These are the things that your consciousness
tries to concentrate on. This is the way that resistance happens in you. Your mind tries to grab hold of one thing. At that
point you must hold your awareness of everything else but
recognize that the one point is producing a resistance. Then
you allow that to happen to you. When you do, the resistance
will tend to disappear or become weaker. The result is that in
your consciousness you will have an increased, more intense,
perception of the relation. You will know the relation in the
same intense way that you might know the breath in your
lungs. Resolving all the conditions and resistances in this way
lets the relationship intensify and the consciousness become
transcendent.

Releasing the conditions that show up is not Sat Nam
Rasayan. That is only a part of the process we use to prepare
to enter the state of Sat Nam Rasayan. It is simple. If you do
not release your resistance, your conditions in the relation,

then there is not enough space for you to have a deeper experience: the intense transcendent experience of the consciousness *in the event.* Your consciousness will remain within the confines of your own individualized, separated self; and there will be no transcendence, no pure and simple state of being.

This all takes practice. It is not something you can hear about and simply incorporate into your life. The recipe is simple but you might not get biscuits on the first try. Keep it up and you will soon find that you are becoming more stable. You will concentrate less and less, allow more and more, and begin to be able to modify what appears. Begin with the coarser resistances: to your physical discomfort, or to a "distracting" sound (remember, there are no distractions in Sat Nam Rasayan). Release the tendency to concentrate your attention on these, and then move on to more subtle resistances, until the very pattern of having resistances is broken and, finally, there simply is no concentration. The effect will be the intensification of your relation with your client or with whatever you are individualizing to. Just remember not to concentrate. Very gently, softly, allow the sensations of the resistance to happen, and the resistance will disappear.

Resistance can take many forms. It is not only when we don't want something to be happening. It is not always a matter of "I don't like this feeling (or that sound, or this disease) and I don't want it to intrude into my space." Only a minority of the resistance that you feel will be like that. Most resistance is more subtle. There is the tiniest judgment, a momentary concentration, or a fleeting fascination with one sensation. Some of your resistance will appear as distraction. This is the sense that something has taken your attention away from the event. But understand that the "distraction" is

The Sacred Space

how you are reacting to this moment in the relation. When you notice this you need to allow it. Don't try to get rid of the distraction or it will continue to be a distraction. Include and allow the sensations of the distraction as you would any other resistance to the relation.

*　*　*

It has begun to snow hard now and I go out of doors to experience the squall more directly. Before my eyes there are millions upon millions of flakes of snow, each different from all the others but each enough alike so that no one of them draws my attention more than any other. In this moment my awareness is equalized. Suddenly, I am ambushed. My daughter throws a snowball at me and I concentrate on that particular bit of snow, larger and more dense, and on a different trajectory than all the rest. Among all the snow, that one bit attracts my attention for a moment. The snowball startles me and so I also have the effects of adrenaline as a part of my experience. The shock of that leads to even more concentration. As I allow these sensations and again become aware of all bits of snow equally, the resistance is released.

When we are healing with Sat Nam Rasayan, sensations are like these snowflakes: countless tiny bits of sensation. Some of the coarser sensations, sensations of discomfort or delight, we concentrate on, like the snowball. This is what we are calling resistance. Resistance is not so much that we are wishing that the delightful or uncomfortable sensations were not there; it is more that the flow of experience, the equal awareness of each moment, each sensation, is being resisted. It is not necessarily resistance born of negativity or anger or fear—it can be much more subtle than that. This resistance can arise out of distraction, interest, or fascination. Some one sensation emerges out of the myriad of sensations and snatches our attention; or perhaps our mind reaches out and grabs at one bit of experience. In any case our mind attaches to that sensation, and that means we experience only that one sensation or related small group of sensations during the duration of the attachment. We neglect everything else. If you don't reduce your resistance, your conditions in the relation, there is not enough space in you to have a deeper experience.

The practice of nonresistance will take time to master. In the beginning all the snowflakes of sensation might receive equal attention only if they are of uniform size and all falling at the same speed and in the same direction. With practice you can learn to keep your inner state stable in relation to the snowflakes of sensation even if some of them are larger or some land right on the end of your nose. Later, with still more practice, you might be able to keep equalized attention even when the snowballs start flying and snowmen and snowwomen begin to appear. Still more practice and you will be stable even in the face of chartreuse and electric blue snowflakes of enormous size, if they should happen to appear.

With an even finer awareness you might notice sensations in response to the infinitely varied crystalline structure of the individual flakes. As you become aware of more and more, you recognize more of the exquisite beauty of all reality, more of the phantasmagoric display of the energies of the universe, more of what has been hidden by your resistance. Most relevant to your purposes as healer, you will become aware of the full richness of the space of the relation between yourself and the client.

The Sacred Space

INDIVIDUALIZING

When we practice in Sat Nam Rasayan, or any other method of healing for that matter, we must choose whom and what we will work with. Our term for that is "to individualize." This means that we are choosing the event with which we will be in relation. In the beginning the whole person of the client is the event. We say that we individualize to the client. A little later you will begin to choose a specific organ, system of the body, chakra, or anything else as your event: whatever it is that needs your healing awareness. If you choose to individualize to your client's digestive system, then every sensation that you have is in relation with that. Imagine yourself in that situation. You have opened the sensitive space, allowed the unending stream of sensations, equalized your awareness, and individualized to your client. As you do this, touching him or her lightly on the arm, you feel a shock of new sensations that you allow and equalize along with all your other sensations. Then you individualize again, this time to the digestive system. Perhaps there is a digestive problem that you want to work with, so you have chosen to individualize there.

As you do this individualization (merely declaring in your consciousness that you are doing so) you will again feel new sensations. These we say are in relation with the digestive system. There is no need to worry as to the cause of the sensations. Do they come from the client's stomach? Do they arise from wherever in your body they are experienced? Do they come from some other source? Do they have any meaning that needs to be interpreted? There is no reason to be concerned with questions like these. You need only to allow these sensations and include whatever appears. If, while you are in relation to the digestive system, a car drives by your house and the sound of that car causes a sensation in you, include that too. If you feel a personal affection for this client, include that sensation. In Sat Nam Rasayan, there are no distractions, and whatever appears is included.

When we individualize, we are simply choosing. I might choose to be in a relation with my client; I might further choose to individualize to her liver. But I do not visualize my client or her liver. That is not necessary and will produce limits in my consciousness, a certain conceptual framework that my sensations will need to squeeze into. What if you wanted to individualize to your client's fear? How would you visualize that? If you made the attempt you would surely be imposing your concepts. It is the same with the physical aspects of our clients. If an image appears, a visual picture of a liver, for example, or a sense of where the liver is, just allow your sensations when that happens. But don't cultivate images. If an image appears it is important to recognize and allow the sensations that arise in you in relation to that image. Until you do, the image is a resistance to the flow of your consciousness and experience. In the same way, don't cultivate sounds or smells or any other sensations. Always avoid imposing your own beliefs or preconceptions about the event onto the actual reality of it.

You can individualize to something you know nothing about. If you have never seen a liver, and don't even know where it is in the body, so much the better. Just say, "I individualize to the liver," and allow whatever shows up. If, on the other hand, you are quite knowledgeable about livers, images and concepts may be almost inevitable for you. If they appear as you individualize, allow the sensations that arise in relation to those images and resolve them as a first step in your treatment process.

When you individualize, the new sensations may appear

anywhere. Individualizing to your client's heart may lead to feelings in your knee or lower back or anywhere else. Several places may experience sensations at once. There is no way to predict this, nor would there be any advantage to being able to do so. Each time you individualize to a heart, it will be different. Heal with your innocence, your ignorance, with a totally fresh view. Otherwise you are putting conditions on the situation, on your client, and on the healing process itself, and conditions can only limit your awareness and effectiveness.

Individualizing in the sensitive space is both simple and easy. If you wish to treat clients, you touch them and enter into a relation with them. You have "individualized" to them and they are now your event. If you wish to be more specific or efficient you might want to individualize to a particular aspect of the client. In your consciousness you would say, "I individualize to his heart chakra," putting this intention into the sensitive space. That is all there is to it. From that point on, your sensations are in relation to the heart chakra and you allow the heart chakra to affect you. Recognize your sensations, allow them, and continue to treat, but now you are treating the heart chakra rather than everything about the client.

When you individualize in the Sacred Space, you are allowing something to affect you, just as when you individualize in the sensitive space. But in the Sacred Space, there is a direct perception of the event you have chosen to individualize to. If you wanted to treat a client's colon you would individualize to it, and when it affected you, you would release the contraction or resistance to its effect until there was no differentiation, no sense of any distance between you and this event.

You get to this point by letting go of the distinction

between the colon and your consciousness. This, too, is simple but in the beginning it is not necessarily easy. It will require some diligent practice for you to be able to hold an object in your perception without feeling that you are looking at it. But this is what needs to be done. Once the event is chosen you will "become one" with the event. That phrase has lost its impact from overuse but it is fairly accurate. You will reduce the differentiation or the sense of distance between you and your event. Subject and object will merge and the perception will be in the event, and you will experience it instead of observing it. Your consciousness and the consciousness in the client's colon become the same. They both appear at the same moment and in the same perceptive space. It is as if your consciousness were happening in the colon.

When you individualize an event in this way, it appears in your perception. The perception is not in your head, it is in the event. When you recognize that the consciousness of the event and your consciousness are exactly the same, then perception and reality appear as one. You feel the event in the event. It is exactly as if you had eyes and ears in the event. This state is a state of nonduality.

When this state of consciousness is applied to your healing you will become very precise and your experience of the event will be very deep and intense. You will recognize the tendencies in the event and know how to modify them. You will have a perception of the event, be it an organ or the client's whole self, as of your own self. In such a moment there is no duality. You don't see a stomach or think about a spleen. There is no witness who looks at the client. Rather, the event appears in your perception as your experience. There might still be a judgment of the event but it appears exactly as your own stomach or spleen or mood might ap-

The Sacred Space

pear to you. It is as if you have another stomach but you know that it is not yours.

Your rational mind may question all this, rebelling against the possibility of knowing what is not seen, tasted, touched, smelled, or heard. But it is a simple thing to experience for yourself. You mustn't be overly eager though. If you are trying too hard, somehow attempting to force the experience, pushing yourself into a concept of what the experience might be like, you will be frustrated. Instead, be sure you have practiced the basics. Put in time each day with the exercises that appear throughout this book. Learn to allow and to equalize, learn to individualize and introduce intention, and then gradually release your propositions, concepts, and prejudgments. This much should pose no problem. All you need do is to keep it up. Eventually you will begin to catch glimpses of the transcendent consciousness of the Sacred Space. It is a slippery place, though, and it is hard to be stable there. When you individualize, you will tend to imagine the event as separate from you. It will take some time before you can hold yourself stable in the space between you and the client. You will be in you, you will in the next moment be in your propositions about your client, and you will flip back and forth between the two. But the Sacred Space is neither of these. Once you find the Space (and here is where working directly with a teacher of Sat Nam Rasayan will be particularly helpful) your progress will accelerate. Knowing what it is you are looking for, instead of just having these words and concepts to guide you, will speed up your progress. When you have individualized to something it will appear in your perception. Instead of feeling how you feel in relation with the stomach or the neck, the stomach or the neck will appear as a part of your perception.

This will then gradually become a part of your normal, everyday experience. The Sacred Space will become such a part of you that it will be automatic for you to perceive there. It will be like learning a new sense, a sense of transcendence. At first you are going to be a bit clumsy with this new sense but in time it will be a natural part of your capabilities. You will use it like any other sense and it will enhance your life. It is very pleasant and interesting and helpful to have this new sense and it will increase enormously your capacity to serve.

TENDENCIES

When you repeatedly react to certain stimuli in a relatively fixed way, that is a tendency. Illness can often be understood as the result of a tendency, a patterned response repeated until damage is done. The conditions of our lives cause us to develop these patterns, both physically and psychologically. When we do healing work we are modifying tendencies in the client. The more conscious you become, the more precise and powerful you will be in your capacity to modify the tendencies of someone who has become stuck in a pattern.

My client Anne was a twin. Her mother apparently resented all the work of caring for two new babies and was not very affectionate toward Anne and her twin brother. As an adult, Anne still has a very limited relationship with her mother and still feels guilt brought on by her mother's chronic complaining, as if her mother's unhappiness were Anne's fault. The patterns of behavior that have resulted have been harmful to Anne. She has not felt free to fully pursue her own happiness and she has suffered accordingly. It is stressful for her to try to plan a vacation, or even a shopping trip. She doesn't feel that she deserves to be happy since her very existence seemed to deny happiness to her mother. The internal struggles she goes through are experienced as tension in her body, and she first came to me suffering from a number of symptoms that are commonly stress related.

Anne had another interesting pattern. As a child, the lack of loving attention from her mother was somewhat relieved by the occasional visits from her mother's older sister, whom Anne fondly remembers as a kindly and attentive aunt. Anne's attraction to this woman has been generalized and Anne has had a number of deep and lasting relationships with older women. This, too, represents a tendency, a way that a behavior (to form a loving relationship) has occurred in response to a stimulus (the presence of a kindly older woman). Anne's attraction has remained quite strong for over four decades. Obviously, not every pattern or tendency is harmful.

Anne demonstrates how patterns and tendencies work. Almost everyone has such tendencies, ways that they repeat patterned behaviors, even though they may sometimes be nonfunctional or harmful. Many patterns are subtle. For example, for some reason my right foot turns out slightly when I walk. It is not the sort of thing that most people would notice. But this has been my tendency for fifty years or so and I have felt some irritation in my right hip as a result. My foot responded to whatever happened to it; its tendency was its way of trying to protect itself, of avoiding some discomfort, as are most tendencies. And now, years later, I have a slight hip problem.

These examples are certainly not unique. Everyone has tendencies: ways that they habitually respond to particular stimuli. Not every tendency is harmful or limiting but they can be, especially if the tendency results in a holding of tension in body or mind. Whenever that happens, whenever a difficult sensation is not attended to and released, whenever pain or fear or sadness or guilt or another hard feeling is held in body or mind, there is tension and the potential for harm, for a limitation of awareness and spontaneity, or for disease.

⚔ RECOGNIZE AND CHOOSE A TENDENCY

Practice now. Tune in. Choose a tendency in your partner (perhaps by simply asking her where she might feel some tension) and begin to research how you might release the resistance that the tendency produces. Do this by equalizing your space and being aware of the feelings in you in relation to the tendency. Allow those feelings. Be fully conscious of them. If you don't feel a sense of completion, a sense that the tendency has been decreased or eliminated, then next recognize what "movement" might modify the consciousness in the event. The movement will most likely be in your consciousness: an intention to reduce the tendency by increasing self-esteem, perhaps, or by decreasing tension. As you introduce the intention, you will feel new sensations. Allow these too until there is completion. If there isn't, and you are a health care practitioner, additional movements might include more physical things: a precise adjustment, an acupuncture needle placement, just the right herb or medication. If you are ready to combine Sat Nam Rasayan with your other expertise, you may simply know what to do. If you don't have that background, or don't feel that you intuitively know what to do, then bring the treatment to completion by continuing to treat in the usual way—expanding, allowing, and equalizing. Even if you don't fully eliminate the tendency in the first treatment, continue to treat until there is some sense of completion, some quieting of your sensations in relation to the event. With continued practice you will know more of how to work with the client's problems, just a bit at a time.

The Sacred Space

This practice session has introduced several new elements for you to work with. I asked you to recognize and choose a tendency, and to make a specific healing movement. I suggested that the movement could be a physical one, and that you may want to include other methods of healing. This is certainly a lot of new material to digest all at once, so you may want to do just one or two of these things. Keep coming back to this particular practice, however, as it represents sophisticated and highly efficient ways of working that you should eventually master. Don't let this intimidate you. Take up the practice of these skills when you feel you are ready.

Any client coming for healing will exhibit a mass of tendencies. Your task is to hold open a space for these tendencies, to allow them, and to "digest" them, if you will. At each session you will digest some more, slowly releasing the client from the grip of his or her tendencies. Not everything has to be completed in one visit. Just let each treatment be complete unto itself.

Your client might have a tendency to worry. The tension of that worry might have led to tightness in his brow and a clenched jaw. This would be a part of how he physically manifests his pattern. Your job is to help release the worry. Go into the Sacred Space. Let your consciousness become transcendent. Anything that happens in the relation between you and the client will manifest in some way. If you want to release the tightness in the brow you will move your awareness through the complex of sensations that come out of this event called the brow, and you will release the resistance you find. This may need to be done over and over, but eventually the tendency for tightness will disappear. Next you might work with the jaw, and finally with the more basic tendency to worry. In some cases, of course, a sickness may not disappear; it is too advanced or the client is not yet able to change that much. But still, much of the tension surrounding the tendency and the illness can be released and the individual healing sessions will feel complete.

What we do in Sat Nam Rasayan is modify tendencies. The more you develop in this system the more capacity you will have to modify the tendencies of someone who is stuck in a pattern. You will change the flow of consciousness just enough for the client to release the tendencies. This occurs whenever you can release all the resistance, because the tendency appears as a contraction, a resistance to the flow of experience, and when that resistance is released, the contraction releases, and the tendency is changed.

A common tendency among healers is to become empathetic. The healer tends to experience the sensation of the client by mirroring the client. It is easy to do this but it is undesirable. Often the beginning healer will treat a client with a headache and wind up with a headache herself. It is simple to avoid this sort of thing. Instead of tending to experience what the client is experiencing, let your intent be to reduce the differentiation or the distance between you and the client. When you do this you will be releasing your conditions and the tendency to be empathetic.

Because of our tendencies, we hardly relate to one another in our everyday affairs. Even in the midst of the most intimate conversations we repeat old patterns based on prior experience with this person or with the people that this person reminds us of. Or, we might relate to how we want this conversation to turn out, or to what we fear in it. It is rare to bring a totally fresh, unprejudiced mind to the relation, as we are learning to do in our system. Instead of being aware, we react, and so we lose an infinity of opportunity, taking in only that little bit that we have left room for. But, when we release

The Sacred Space

these tendencies and conditions and resistances, the relation can suddenly become very intense. When it does and we are stable, the consciousness can become transcendent, even in everyday circumstances.

When we individualize or accept someone or something in relation with us we feel the reaction that we have been calling the shock. These reactions come out of our tendencies and the conditions that we place on the relation. "I need to know this person's name, her intent, whether she wishes to shake my hand or not, her opinion of me, and her willingness to help." All kinds of conditions. "She is beautiful; she is like my sister; she is so boring; I wish she would stop calling me." All of this is felt somewhere in our bodies. This is what we call the shock. Sometimes it is almost violent; often it is very subtle. In any case, when we experience the shock in our everyday consciousness, it tends to rule us. Instead of being in direct relation with the object of our experience, we wind up in relation to the shock produced by our conditions and tendencies.

As a healer, some shocks occur when we see a client and have the feeling that we will not be able to help him. Maybe he seems resistant, maybe we don't like the cut of his clothes, or maybe his illness seems too severe for us to be of much use. We frame a position in relation to this person that is almost unresolvable. That frame, those tendencies, limit us. Sometimes a client tells us, after we have treated him, that some illness, one he had never mentioned to us, is clearing up. If we had known ahead of time that he was sick in that way we might have thought ourselves incapable of helping. We thought he was just concerned about his headaches and we thought, "Good, for me headaches are no problem." But the headache was just the tip of the iceberg. The client's entire life was a mess, he was falling apart, but we didn't know that and so we were able to avoid our own tendency and we didn't put him in the category of "unhelpable."

Please recognize that many of these tendencies and conditions are unavoidable. Whatever your spiritual or emotional status you will create them. No matter what you do you will have some of these resistances to your own experience. But we can turn their existence to our advantage. We can work with them, and then they are not a problem at all, they are a part of our process. We allow them. We recognize what is happening, we recognize the shock and we play a game with the shock as a method of getting to the state of no differentiation, no tendency. This will give us the possibility of seeing without the filters, transcending everyday consciousness, and healing with our presence. The consequences are enormous.

KNOWING

One of our objects in Sat Nam Rasayan is direct knowledge of the event. Up until now we've been primarily concerned with recognizing our sensations in relation to an event and working with those sensations. But we can go further than that. We can know the event itself, directly, with the same clarity that we know our own sensations. This is not the knowing of a subject by an observer, but it is knowledge without any distinction between subject and object, between the knower and the known. Knowledge of this sort is sacred and is necessary if we are to consider our system complete. This is the experience of the Sacred Space.

In intuition, the very first experience is knowledge. Intuition is not a matter of gathering data and bringing the data together and then drawing a conclusion. It is just the opposite. With intuition you begin with the conclusion and then, if you need to communicate, even to communicate within your own mind, the conclusion is massaged by the intellect into a model, so that a statement can be made about your experience. You have an experience in the space of intuition and, if it needs to be translated, if, for example, a diagnosis is called for, the "intelligent process" is used and the conclusion is put into words.

In the beginning with Sat Nam Rasayan we do not bother ourselves too much with this. We can do without diagnosis, which would not be possible in many other forms of healing. In allopathic medicine this would be totally unacceptable. In medicine, a diagnosis is always sought before treatment is begun. Sometimes it is not possible to know what a disease is and the patient is treated symptomatically, especially if there is a need for emergency measures, but in general a diagnosis is sought. With Sat Nam Rasayan it is different because we are simply relating to our sensations, and if the sensations are resolved, we know that the tendencies have been modified appropriately and the treatment is complete.

Many who come to Sat Nam Rasayan as students have a very analytic intelligence. Westerners tend to think in linear cause-and-effect sequences when they try to understand disease and bring about healing. That is certainly the case in allopathic medicine and it is also true of much of our psychological and even psychic and energetic healing. The mode of thinking goes something like this: since (A) has happened to this person, the result has been (B). If we are to get rid of the problem (B) we will have to alter the condition by applying a force (C). But in Sat Nam Rasayan our thinking is quite different. We work with the intelligence of synthesis rather than analysis. This sort of intelligence works more with relations than with cause and effect. If, using synthetic intelligence, you wished to speak of a heron on a riverbank, you would have to speak, not of an isolated creature, but of the river, the relation of the heron to the river, the relation of the river to the forest, the relations among all the other animals and plants and bacteria and molds in the heron's ecosystem, and so on. There is no beginning and no end to the web of relations. The synthesis of all the relations is the truer picture of the heron. Without the synthesis and the relations it is really impossible to describe the bird. Without the web of relations it is impossible for the heron to exist.

In Sat Nam Rasayan, and in an increasing number of other areas of thought and consciousness, we are working more with synthesis and relations than with cause and effect. Our clients are not examined as objects, or even as a patient might be examined and treated by a physician. The physician is looking for certain signs and symptoms that the patient has, for a disease that can be named, and for its cause and treatment: because of (A), the patient has condition (B), so it is time to institute therapy (C). In our system, we do not say that the client *has* a condition but rather that a certain quality exists *in relation to* the client. The allopathic physician diagnoses and defines the disease (and, therefore, to some extent the patient) by signs and symptoms. He has fever, weight loss, malaise, and painful and frequent urination, so this is probably a urinary tract patient and, therefore, certain further tests or treatments are called for. But in Sat Nam Rasayan we need to do it in a synthetic way. It will not work for us to say, "This patient has this or that particular disease, so I will do this treatment." The scientific, analytic mind wants this, but for us it is no good. We need to have an experience of the object.

In Sat Nam Rasayan, either you *know*, in which case the

"diagnosis" is made and the treatment can be completed, or there is *resistance*. You know that you don't know because a condition appears in your sensitive space. Right now, you know that you are reading a book. But if you stated to someone that you were reading, if you even thought it, that would be a condition or concept, a moment of resistance to the flow of experience and therefore a moment of not knowing. When you make the statement that you are reading, the statement appears in consciousness as a concept and a resistance. When we experience something we tend to put our concepts over it, and those concepts are felt in the sensitive space as resistance. When you experience the resistance, then you know that you don't know; you know that, in place of knowing, in place of a pure and direct experience of reality, you have a concept. When you experience something, you tend to put your presuppositions over it, and that is what you feel in the sensitive space.

⚔ RECOGNIZE AND RELEASE CONCEPTS

With your partner, tune in, open your space, equalize, and then individualize to the stomach. Immediately notice how you might think *about the stomach: where you see it, at what distance from you it seems to be, what it looks like, and so on. These are all your concepts. Your job is to recognize what it feels like to have these concepts, to recognize the concepts themselves, and to release them. Feel your sensations in relation to each concept. Allow these sensations while remaining aware of all other sensations. As you allow them, the effects of having a concept will diminish and soon the concept itself will disappear from your consciousness. Then another may appear, along with its sensations, and you will repeat the process. Take your time now and do that with each of your concepts in turn. After a short time the very pattern of having concepts about the*

stomach will be broken and you will be much closer to a direct
experience of the consciousness in the stomach.

If you wish to learn to diagnose, if you wish to exercise your intuition, you will need to try not to translate your stomach thoughts into conclusions about the stomach. More to the point you will need to not even have your stomach thoughts. What is left if there are no thoughts about the stomach? The answer is the stomach itself. Then there would be no distance, no separation or boundary, between you and the stomach. Your experience would be direct and you would simply know the consciousness in the stomach. To your analytical mind it may seem that there is a step missing here. How did we get from "no concepts" to "direct experience"? How does that happen? What is the bridge? There is no bridge. You are here and then you are there. And, for better or worse, nothing more can be said.

DIAGNOSIS

Until now I have used the word "resistance" to refer to all resistance that might be experienced during healing, and I have made no differentiation among possible sources of resistance. If you were working with your sister as a client and she was suffering with tension in her neck, you would experience resistance as you individualized to her neck. In our work up until now, the process would have you simply release the resistance that you experienced, without giving any thought to its source. But in that case there would be no way to tell if the resistance was in you or in your sister's neck. You would have come to this session with a great many preconceptions about your sister. You've shared much of her per-

The Sacred Space

sonal history, you have clear images of her in your mind, you know her well. You may also have both positive and negative feelings about her, and opinions as to the source of her tension. All these preconceptions or concepts about her, and many more as well, will produce resistance. Again "resistance" is referring not to your personal opinions about your sister but to the more subtle blocks to your full experience of the reality of her in this moment. Some of these blocks, or resistances, may be born of your opinions, but others may come from nothing more insidious than a sense of her physical position in relation to you as you treat her.

Resistance appearing in your sensitive space could also come from your sister's neck. If you have been successful in reducing the resistances that are due to your own preconceptions, what you would then experience as resistance would be the result of your awareness of the experience of the consciousness in her neck. This would represent an important milestone in your evolution as a healer. If you can tell the difference between the resistance that comes from your concepts and the resistance in the event, you are getting close to diagnosis. Please understand that this does not mean that you will be able to say, "This patient has staphylococcal pneumonia," or, "The cause of your hepatitis is an immunodeficiency due to . . . " That sort of diagnosis requires medical knowledge that you may not have. That is the diagnosis that essentially is the naming of the disease, an important step in successful medical treatment, but not a critical element in Sat Nam Rasayan.

Our diagnosis is different. We are endeavoring to have a direct experience of the event, to reduce all distance between the event and the healer. Through that transcendent knowledge of the event the diagnosis can be made. It would actually risk reestablishing the distance or differentiation if the disease were to be named. It would tend to re-create the point of view of the healer. This is not necessarily the case but it is likely, especially in the early stages of growth in Sat Nam Rasayan.

On the other hand, if you are a healer in Sat Nam Rasayan as well as a physician or other medically trained healer, you might, for example, upon individualizing to a patient's liver, simply recognize a disturbance of bilirubin metabolism. If you did not have such a background your experience in the liver might be more of a "congestion." So a lot depends on your background, on what else you know. The trouble arises when we come to the liver with our conceptions of it intact. Then we will be examining it as if from outside, from a point of view. Then we will be trying to interpret what we experience, to give a name to it. If a physician well experienced in Sat Nam Rasayan were to work on the liver, she might have no interpretation whatsoever for her experience there. She might feel congestion and "know" that more water was needed. She might introduce an intention to increase the water element in the liver and complete her treatment without ever considering the name of what she was treating. On the other hand, she might intuitively or rationally recognize the metabolism disorder, treat it with Sat Nam Rasayan, and later on perform tests and institute standard medical treatments. In a similar manner an herbalist treating the same client might "know" that the client needs to use an infusion of dandelion to enhance liver function. But knowledge in Sat Nam Rasayan, diagnosis as we use this term, is simply there, it does not need to be deduced from the evidence. While your rational or analytic mind might reel from such a proposition, it is perfectly legitimate to the intuitive, synthesizing mind.

The Sacred Space

Consider your actual experience with this. If you are a parent you know if your child is sad. There is an instant recognition of that. You do not need to ponder the meaning of the signs and symptoms of sadness, nor psychologically analyze the causes of the sadness. You may not even think that he is sad, but may immediately, thoughtlessly, draw your child to you and kiss his forehead. In other words, you have been in a sensitive space in relation to your child—have experienced a resistance in him, diagnosed, and in this case treated him, all without any internal dialogue.

In a treatment situation, imagine you have individualized to your client's liver. Do you have an idea or an image about where her liver is or what it looks like? These are your concepts and will produce resistance to deeper experience. When you individualize to an event such as the liver, notice all the presuppositions you have about it. Where do you imagine it is, what shape do you see it having, what is its color or size? Realize that you have all these concepts and that each of them produces sensations in you. Allow these sensations, continue to equalize your space, and each resistance will re solve. What will be left is the experience of the liver. What stays, after you have resolved your own resistances due to your preconceptions, is the experience of the consciousness in the event, in this case, the liver. If you haven't resolved the resistances, you don't have an experience of the event. It is as if you are looking at a boat moored offshore in a thick fog. The boat is there but your vision of it is obscured.

The process of resolving your own resistances so that you can have a clear experience of the consciousness in the event is important for your efficiency as a healer. As I write these words on my computer I am able to go directly to each letter that I want to use. What if, instead of a keyboard, I had a device that required me to start at the beginning of the alphabet and go through all the letters until I got to the one I wanted to use? If I wanted to type a *G*, I would have to go through *A,B,C,D,E*, and *F*. I would eventually get to the *G* but the process would be inefficient. That is the way it is in Sat Nam Rasayan at the stage we are describing. You will need to recognize and resolve your resistance A, resistance B, resistance C, and so on until you finally arrive at resistance G, the one in the event itself. It works, but it is inefficient. With practice, however, you will be able to go more directly to the consciousness in the event to resolve the resistance there, and your healing will be much more efficient.

Practice going through your resistances as described above and learn to hold yourself absolutely stable, to make no movements in your consciousness at all. This is a step toward making your efficiency even greater. By being stable in your consciousness and knowing the consciousness in the event, you will know exactly where the conditions in the event can be modified or released. You will know what is needed and you will make the specific movement that causes the appropriate change. If, for example, you were working on your client's jaw, you would open the space, quickly release your own resistances (perhaps growing out of your visualization of her jaw), and experience the consciousness in the jaw. You would hold yourself stable and research the jaw. You might find a line of contraction running from the right masseter muscle down toward the left sternocleidomastoid muscle in her neck (although you might not know the names of those structures). You would then research further and discover that a release in the fourth vertebral area would help. Then you would release it and research some more. You might next discover a further movement, a stimulation, needed under

The Sacred Space

the tongue. That movement, the stimulation, might complete the treatment. The whole process could take only a minute.

What has happened in all this? An analogy might help. If I am meditating, I will know, without thought, the experience in my shoulder. If I notice a sensation of discomfort there I can allow the sensation or I can recognize that a slight shift in my posture will release the pressure. Once I have made that shift, my awareness shows a further tendency in my back, and another movement, perhaps a relaxation, will modify that. All of this could take place in a few seconds. There is nothing at all mysterious in any of this. We all do it all the time, although we are usually not conscious of what we are doing and so we may be inefficient in our movements.

This is a fair analogy to the healing process when you are in the Sacred Space. You "know" the tendency, you "know" the movement required, and you "know" when the process is complete. But the movements in Sat Nam Rasayan need not be physical and are, in fact, generally movements in consciousness. What is known may not be easily put into words; and, most interestingly, the event is not one's own shoulder but another person's. But the analogy is correct despite these differences. When you are in the Sacred Space, the consciousness in your event is as real as the consciousness in your own shoulder.

In the diagnosis and treatment process, you are looking for the vital point in the relation, that one bit that can be moved with the result that everything can balance. Your experience produces in you a kind of image of the event, not a visual image, but the synthetic, nonanalytic imprint of your experience. You will know in that image or imprint what the vital point is and how the event can be most efficiently modified.

To arrive at this, research, identify, and release your

propositions or concepts so that you can learn the difference between your own resistances and the resistances caused by the event itself. Do this and you will come to a state of knowing. Then find the vital point and make the appropriate movement to release the conditions in the event. I recognize that this may be getting a bit obscure and ahead of your current ability. If you are having difficulty following these words it may mean that it is time once again to stop reading and do more practice. These teachings need to be absorbed slowly over time.

THE ELEMENTS

WE HAVE SPOKEN of healing as balance, but, you might ask, "Balance of what?" You may think in terms of psychological balance and imagine one who is healed as having become free of neurosis or unreasonable fear or desire. Or you may recognize the need for physical balance, a state of vibrant good health based on exercise, flexibility, healthful diet, and restorative sleep. Or perhaps you understand healing as a spiritual balance in which you are able to recognize and serve the divine in all, while retaining a neutral state of mind. Yet another way to understand balance is in terms of the overarching system of the "elements" of earth, water, fire, air, and ether.

These elements represent five qualities of body and mind that need to be in balance if one is to know peace in living and dying. You can work with these elements in your Sat Nam Rasayan practice. The process in its simplest form is to open the sensitive space, individualize to an event, and then hold the intention that one or another of the elements be in balance in the event. Upon doing this you will feel new sensations in relation to that intention. Allow these sensations until the resistances that engendered them are resolved. This is a simple extension of what you have practiced up to now and should not be too much of a challenge.

Later you will know more about which element to balance and if it needs to be increased or decreased, but in the beginning just choose an element and hold to the simple intention that the element be balanced in the event. This will prevent any possible negative side effects. If, for example, a client was very angry (a fiery quality) you would only need to intend that the fire element be balanced, without having to consider whether to increase it or decrease it. With experience you might know to hold an intention of reducing the fire element or the value of increasing the water element as an antidote to too much fire, but in the beginning, stick with simply balancing the elements and you can't go wrong. You can also intend that each of the elements, in turn, be balanced. This will be very effective and foolproof, although it is inefficient compared to just balancing the elements that need to be balanced. As you begin your practice with the elements, however, this may be what feels safest to you. However you start working with the elements, just be sure to research the effect of your intent. Notice how your movements in consciousness are affecting the event. In this way you will become more secure in your practice and more efficient.

EARTH

Earth is the element of our roots, our support: solid, strong, still, and grounded. This is the beginning, the base, of everything material. As the element of support, earth relates to our bones and joints, our feet, our legs, and the sciatic nerve. The earth element is the element of the first chakra, or energy center, located at the perineum and the coccyx at the base of the spine. Red, the color with the slowest vibration, is the color of the earth element. Earth is solid and condensed, and the way we experience the earth is through its support and through gravity.

The earth element, like all the elements, must be in balance if we are to be in balance. When it is, we feel secure. We feel able to meet our basic survival needs and ensure our material prosperity. When this element is strong in us we know what we require and we can do whatever is necessary to fulfill our needs.

When the earth element is feeble we feel insecurity—a feeling that we encounter as intemperance and self-indulgence, depression, unresolved grief, or selfishness. Physically, when we are unstable or unbalanced in the earth element, we might suffer from obesity, hemorrhoids, constipation, or arthritis.

▨ RELATE TO THE EARTH ELEMENT

Take time now to be aware of your sensations as you relate to the earth. Seat yourself solidly, firmly. Close your eyes, tune in, and open the sensitive space. Begin to become aware of the various sensations in your body. Notice, without comment, all your sensations. Be aware of the more obvious sensations: points of discomfort, the pressure of your legs against your cushion, the effects of sounds that go through you. Notice with equal awareness more subtle sensations: the feeling of air passing through your nostrils and over your skin, and the flutter of a muscle as it relaxes or tenses. Notice as well even more delicate sensations, such as the nameless energies concealed in every tissue. Go into the spaces between those sensations and discern still more. But equalize your attention so that each sensation receives the same attention as all the others, regardless of its intensity. Recognize that all the sensations of this moment

*are occurring at the same time, not in a sequence of one sensation
and then another and then another. Do all this by not doing, by
letting go of all effort and all concentration. Let no one sensation
reach out and snatch your interest. In this way become stable in the
sensitive space of Sat Nam Rasayan.*

*Then, without losing your awareness of these sensations, also
choose to be aware of the sensations in you that seem to arise out of
your relation to the gravity of the earth. Sitting as you are, recognize that you do not actually feel the earth but rather you feel the
effects of gravity. You do not know the earth; you know of its effect
on you. Be tuned into those effects. Feel the sensations as gravity
draws on you. Notice it everywhere, in your legs, in the skin of your
face, and in your internal organs. Simply allow those sensations to
be there, as they are, without judgment or concentration. Also notice
where you don't notice the pull of gravity, and equally allow the
feeling of that. Throughout, continue to allow all other sensations
and include any and all new sensations that might arise. Allow all
and equalize your awareness.*

Spend time with this practice. Research for yourself the
experience of your relation to the earth. Later you will be
able to modify the space of the relation between you and
your client by modifying the earth element in that relation.
For now just get to know the ever-changing kaleidoscope of
sensations in relation to the earth.

I have given hints about what the sensations in relation to
the earth might be, but I don't want you to explore this or
any of the other elements with preconceived notions. When
you work with a client it is central to the entire Sat Nam
Rasayan process to be completely objective. If you are
searching for a particular sensation, trying, for example, to
discern the heaviness of the earth, you will be resisting the

flow of your actual experience. So, even though you might spend some time becoming sensitive to the effects of the earth's gravity, or coming to an awareness of the nature of another element, the purpose of this is only to help you understand the place of these elements in your constitution. Practice with them, read and think about them, but then let go of all your ideas about them. Perhaps when you introduce an intention to balance the earth element in a client, the sensations that you will feel will be of lightness or of heat. It will be necessary for you to recognize these sensations and to allow them as easily as you would allow a heavy sensation of gravity pulling on you.

⚒ INTRODUCE AN INTENTION

When you are done with the meditation on the earth, notice how you feel. Notice the effect of having been aware of the earth element. You might expect a sense of groundedness, relaxation, and security, an enhanced sense of self and identity. But let your research be objective, without even these expectations. As a further exercise, this time with a partner, again open the sensitive space. As usual, tune in and then stabilize your space by equalizing your sensations. After touching your partner's arm, allow all the sensations of the new relation and equalize again. Don't concentrate— allow everything equally and continue to treat your partner for a few minutes more. Then release into the space of the relation the intention that the earth element shall be balanced in your partner.

The insertion of an intention into the space of the relation is a delicate process. Using a quiet inner voice, state your intention in simple terms. Actual words are not required but neither are they a hindrance to the process. Intention is a thought, a purpose, a goal, but not an effort or an action of any kind. It is a dainty thing, refined, never forceful or labored. Putting intention into a relation is as gentle as if a piece of downy fluff were on the palm of your hand and you blew it off and allowed it to float in the space around you. Once the intention is there it needs to be maintained, but that is an equally gentle thing.

Gently launch that sort of intention. Intend that the earth element will be balanced and then remove your own will from the picture and experience whatever sensations arise. As always, allow the new sensations, equalize them, and continue to be aware of all your other sensations as well. Treat your partner for a few minutes in this way, or until you feel an impression of completion.

WATER

Water is the element associated with flow: the flow of emotions, of pleasure, of sexuality. Water is the non-doer, the force that seems to yield to every obstacle, but eventually can wear through the densest rock or the hardest steel. Water is the element of the second chakra, located midway between the pubis and the navel, the home of creativity, sexuality, and stored energy. This is the region of the uterus, genitals, kidneys, and bladder—organs closely linked with water. When the water element is out of balance, too strong or too weak, disturbances such as impotence, frigidity, or urinary tract problems can result. Emotionally, a water imbalance might appear as an inability to feel or express emotion, as fear or anxiety, or as attachment, excessive or decreased sexual desire, or a sense of frustration.

Water in balance means that we can be fluid and flexible in both the movements of our bodies and the manifestations of our desires. Desire motivates movement, whether that desire is for more cash or for cosmic consciousness. Desire in turn is rooted in pleasure, which is an essential motivator. Without our urge for pleasure, we would have little motivation to heal, to elevate our spirit, to develop deeper relationships, or to increase material wealth. The fluid nature of our urges means that they can easily lead to self-indulgence on the one hand or avoidance of pleasure on the other, depending on our inner tendencies. Sexuality may be a balanced expression of love, affection, and reproductive urges or it may become repressed, exploitative, or perverted, again depending on our inner tendencies. The water element, like water itself, shapes itself to fit the container we carry it in.

To begin to enhance your awareness of the nature of the water element and your sensations in relation to it, play with water. Let tapwater run over your hands, swim and dive, drink lots of water and feel it in your stomach, go without water for a while to get to know the effect of that, or fill a balloon with water and feel its fluid nature. In each case experience your sensations in relation to the water, not so as to memorize these sensations, but rather simply to be keenly aware of them. As with the earth element, the intent is to heighten your awareness of the existence and workings of the water element.

◢ RELATE TO THE WATER ELEMENT

As you did with the earth element, now meditate on water. Tune in and open the sensitive space. Be aware of and allow all your sensations. Equalize and become stable. After a while feel the presence of water in you. Let this happen by doing nothing more than simply intending to be conscious of the water element. You need not imagine water or remember having played in it or in any other way conjure up an image or memory of water. Instead just feel the presence of the water element in you, in this moment.

Feel your own fluidity, the experience of being made up mostly of water. Feel the less fluid: your bones and teeth; as well as the more fluid: your saliva and blood circulation. Also be sensitive to the way that impressions and emotions "flow" through your mind. Be aware of all your sensations and allow them. Equalize your space. Then let your intention be that the water element be balanced in you. Immediately, as you release this intention into your sensitive space, notice all the new sensations that may arise. Allow these as well. Once again equalize your awareness. Continue in this manner for a few minutes more.

Now practice with a partner. Open the space, allow all your sensations, equalize, and then touch his or her arm. Feel the shock of new sensations and allow them, equalizing once again. Become quite stable. Eschew concentration. Treat your partner for a few minutes, continuing to stabilize the space of your relation. Now introduce the intention that the water element will be balanced. Recognize and allow all the sensations that arise in relation to your intention. One might especially want to balance the water element if a client's emotions are not flowing, if there are emotional blocks to be released.

FIRE

Combustion. Heat. The inferno. The lustrous gem of the third chakra located at the solar plexus. The pancreas, adrenals, liver, spleen, and digestive system. Metabolism, movement, and transformation. Matter transformed into energy, and inertia into action. Personal power, will, and motivation. Anger, guilt, greed, and doubt.

Fire. The word is filled with overtones of meaning: enthusiasm, passion, intensity, fervor, fever, to be fired up, the hot emotion of anger, fiery words to incite or inspire another. There are those with too much fire, and those with not enough. There are aspects of us in which fire should dominate, there are other aspects where too much fire is not useful. Like all qualities, there is a balance that serves, and imbalances that can harm.

The element of fire gives us the ability to rise above judgment and our attachment to personal desires. Fire is the midwife of will, and the offspring of mind and action. When in balance, fire doesn't give raw power with which to dominate and control but rather the power to integrate and create wholeness. An appropriate dose of fire gets things done. It is essential in developing a sense of identity in the world. It lets us use our will to consciously control change. This is power with responsibility, the power to forge our own circumstances, the power to build a better world. Too much or too little fire can lead to depression, doubt, anger, greed, guilt, a sense of being a victim, or a thirst for power.

A balance of the fire element will manifest as an ability to set goals and achieve them. It will be noted as personal energy and motivation levels that are strong but not manic. Balance of fire is expressed as self-confidence, the ability to make decisions, the ability to inspire others, and the capacity to learn from everyday life. Physically, imbalances in the fire element may manifest as ulcers, gallstones, jaundice, hepatitis, diabetes or hypoglycemia, or other disturbances of the third chakra organs of digestion, metabolism, and cleansing.

⚔ RELATE TO THE FIRE ELEMENT

Learning to work with the fire element is not unlike learning to work with any other element. Think of people you know who are fiery or who seem to lack fire. Meditate on the feeling of fire as you experience it in yourself, whether it might seem strong, weak, or in appropriate balance. Sense the heat of your own metabolism. Then, with a partner, tune in and open the sensitive space. When you are stable, introduce the intention of balancing the fire element. Recognize the shock of new sensations in relation to your intention, and continue to treat until there is a sense of completion.

AIR

Air is the element associated with the fourth, or heart, chakra. The dominant quality of air is its ability to disperse, to expand and fill whatever space it might occupy. Air is associated with breath and spirit, energy, love, and life force. It has no set form. It moves freely. Love is like that: true love has no limits.

When this element is in balance one can be compassionate and have the ability to give where giving is called for; relationships are rewarding; and there is health in the area of the heart and lungs. Without a balance of the air element one may find it hard to know or express one's own emotions or may have difficulty being sensitive to the feelings of others. One may be afraid to give or may foolishly give to those who would exploit. Balancing the air element is also one way to treat pain.

◢ RELATE TO THE AIR ELEMENT

Feel air moving in and through you. Feel it moving over your skin. Feel the power of a strong wind and the soothing quality of a gentle breeze. Know your breath and the energy that comes to you with the air you breathe. Become intimate with the breath. Spend time breathing slowly, deeply, and very deliberately, feeling the air expanding in you as you inhale, and feeling relaxation and release as

The Elements

you exhale. Imagine that you can feel the breath dispersing into and energizing every cell in your body, and that you can feel the exhalation carrying unwanted tension out of you. Sense how the breath connects you to all other life, how the air that moves through you also moves through all plants and animals and circulates over our entire planet, connecting you to all other living things.

With a partner, tune in, open, and stabilize your space in the usual manner. Then introduce the intention that the air element be in balance. Experience and allow any sensations that arise and treat to completion. If you want to increase the air element in your client find one of the qualities of air that you can recognize, say the feeling of air moving across your skin, and be aware of that. Find it in yourself and hold that sensation. This will increase the air element in the relation.

ETHER

This is the element of purification associated with the fifth chakra, located at the throat. Ether is the element of communication, emptiness, dreams, and transcendence, and of going beyond all physical form. It is in the ether that we really communicate, express, connect, and inspire. Ether is the element of ecstasy. Ether is the means by which consciousness can extend itself and by which all interconnects with all. Ether is how we go beyond all the boundaries that apply to the more dense elements. This is the realm of pure idea and direct knowing. Ether is associated with a much finer energy than any of the other elements and is the element of formlessness.

Mastery of ether implies a mastery of self. With a balance of this element distractions of the world are never a problem, and the meditative mind can master the emotions. When the ether element is balanced one will seek higher truth, beyond the limitations of time and space, beyond cultural conditioning, beyond circumstances.

◢ RELATE TO THE ETHER ELEMENT

With a partner as your client, tune in, open the sensitive space, and meditate on the feeling of emptiness. Recognize the feeling of the emptiness of the space in which you sit and allow that sensation to happen to you. Don't visualize the emptiness but simply recognize it in your sensations. Feel your sensations and then feel the sensations between the sensations and the sensations between them. Eventually feel the empty space between the sensations. Do the same with your thoughts: be aware of the spaces between your thoughts. This space is like the emptiness of outer space: it is vast compared to the relatively tiny planets and stars that occupy it. When you are stable, touch your partner lightly on the arm, feel the shock of new sensations, and equalize again. Then introduce the intention to balance the ether element in your partner. As with all intentions, research the sensations in relation to it and allow them until the treatment feels complete.

In general, if you increase the ether element in a client, he or she will sleep. If you sense emptiness while individualizing your client's navel point (the third chakra), this will deeply relax your client and release anger. If you introduce a little ether at the first chakra it will help people to feel less restricted, but too much ether there might cause them to feel insecure.

Balancing elements can now become a part of your repertoire as a healer. Gradually research the effects of intentions

The Elements

to balance one or more of the elements in your partner. In the beginning of your work with elements it is perfectly acceptable to simply balance each of them in turn, noticing the effects of this in your sensitive space. Later, with more experience, you'll only work with the elements that need balancing. Finally, you'll be able to intentionally increase or decrease the strength and influence of individual elements as needed.

LOVE

ONCE I had a belief that was so enormous that it filled my entire consciousness, and I could not see it as a belief but thought my belief was the only reality. It was as if I had lived my entire life in a deep cave, never seeing the light of day. By dim candlelight I studied my lessons and mastered many things but I knew nothing, absolutely nothing, of the larger world, not even of its existence. This cave was my world, my universe. Finally I was led out, into the daylight, and to this day I remain dazzled by what there is to see and know in the wide world. I will never lose sight of the beauty of this world of ours; never will I forget to appreciate its richness. Only, I wonder, might this be another cave? Might there be one more emerging yet to come, or a thousand?

In the cave of my everyday awareness I had always believed that I was "here" at this point, and that everything else was "there," more or less separated from me. My point of view was just that, a point, the I in the very center of all else. From my point of view I looked out at events. The fullness in my stomach after a meal was not at that point of view any more than was the sun or the moon. My consciousness and the events of which I was conscious were different and forever separate. Some immutable law made it so. My belief in that law was so pervasive that I could not see it as a belief. It enclosed me as a cave, and my entire life was lived within its confines.

Emerging from the cave I learned for the first time that it was possible to reduce the differentiation between event and consciousness, to reduce it completely. When I did I was dazzled by the experience of the consciousness in the event. "I" dissolved and this consciousness became like an ocean of consciousness continually receiving, without filter, millions upon millions of new drops of reality. The experience is of an endless phantasm of pure love.

This love I feel is in being in an absolute relation to an event instead of in a limited relation. How would you feel if you were invited to your friend's house for a talk, and when you began your conversation your friend turned on the television set and then called another friend on the telephone? This is the state of most of our relations: divided, with attention here, there, and everywhere. It is as if we were victimized by our own subconscious, which takes us first to one thing and then to another, reacting to this and that, totally unstable and almost never in a sustained, intense relation with anything.

Learn how to be more and more aware and how to be stable in your neutral mind, your meditative mind. Learn to hold the equalization of awareness for a long time. It can only happen with practice. You must become empty, and this will not happen by thinking about it. Practice opening the sensitive space, as I have described, and keeping it equalized. Our problem is that this way of healing is based on the neutral mind, and words don't well describe such a state: it is best experienced through your practice.

Love

⚔ INDIVIDUALIZE AND EQUALIZE

Practice again now. Tune in, open the space, and equalize. Then individualize to an event, any event, and equalize again. Do this over and over, individualizing and equalizing, individualizing and equalizing. Hold open the possibility that your point of view, your sense of a distance between you and your event, will diminish and eventually you will be free of this limitation altogether. This is not just the way to heal; it is also the way to live in bliss and peace. It will feel as if your awareness is expanded. If you can do this without producing tendencies, it is like living without fear or attachment—you will feel very elevated and you will be a great healer.

When you individualize it is easy to redevelop that old feeling of having a point of view with its preferences and perspectives. This exercise will help you to not do that—but remember, it is hard to drop the pattern of having a viewpoint. You will likely find that you are rather attached to your sense of self. It is like being deeply in love and then being asked to just let it go. You have developed this strong tendency to hold to a point of view, but the job for right now is to release the reference point so that you can become more neutral. At the very least learn when you are neutral and when you are not. When you can recognize your own instability you will be able to deal with it. By this point in your practice you have probably recognized that at the moment you begin to concentrate, you become unstable and tend to come out of the Space. You should also recognize whenever you begin to produce a tendency. You need to know this because these tendencies will modify your event, your client, as surely as an intention would. You need to have the capacity to stop your tendencies whenever you choose. If you are not stable you should be able to recognize that and deal with it. This will give you greater peace in your life and help you to heal both yourself and others.

We are seeking a state of neutrality: a state that has been emptied of all conditions, and to some this might feel frightening. But neutrality is neither oblivion nor bland detachment; it is rather the way to an intense involvement, and this is quite pleasant and most important to our healing purposes. Moreover, it is out of this condition-less state of awareness that true compassion and love can emerge. If your awareness is not empty, if you have in it a sense of self, of the point of view we keep mentioning, then there are also the judgments that go with that, and in judgment there is no love.

Consider this ego-free state called love. In it, whatever is present is fully allowed, without evaluation and without judgment. Love is not a great deal of affection; it is a state beyond affection. In the state of love, if something is, if it exists, it is allowed. Everything that appears in awareness is included without discrimination, and no separation is created. Without boundaries there is no place where I must put up my defenses and make my choices about what to allow in and what to exclude from consciousness. Real compassion and love begin with this allowing of whatever appears within the self. If one is able to know and allow one's own experience, then, by extension, one is able to allow whatever or whoever has engendered that experience. That is love. That is absolute compassion. And that is the essence of a healing presence.

This love is not blind—far from it. When one is truly sensitive, one is keenly aware of how a relation with another is affecting one's experience and is not likely to tolerate either the obnoxious or the evil. Nor will one who is sensitive

Love

tolerate his or her own negative behavior. Allowing is not synonymous with permitting. When we allow we experience fully, without filters of either fear or desire. That full experience is precisely what makes us intolerant of whatever is doing harm. Our first choice is to heal the harmful. If that cannot happen we may choose, with awareness intact, to move away from the harmful or, if necessary, to defend ourselves or others against harm, by whatever means necessary. Being aware, allowing, and loving do not imply being a victim.

✍ Individualize with a Partner

Go back now to actual practice. With a partner go through a process of individualizing, dropping the individualization, equalizing, then individualizing again, and so on. You could, for example, tune in, open the space, equalize, and then individualize to the feet, equalizing in the space of the relation to the feet. Then drop the individualization of the feet and equalize again. Then go to the lower legs, equalize in the space of the relation, drop the individualization, equalize, go on to the knees, and so on right through the entire body. At each region, feel the shock of sensations as you let the space of the relation affect you, equalize, and then move on. The same thing could be done with the chakras (see the chapter on chakras), or with the different elements. At each point along the way recognize when your state is totally stable, when, that is, you are fully present in a state of love.

LETTING GO
OF PREJUDICE

B Y NOW you can be completely equalized, your consciousness empty. At first there is no movement, but
then some tendency appears. Develop the capacity to
drop the tendency, to stop it from happening, so that you remain stable in your space. In the exercise above, notice how
you might have ideas about each of the parts that you individualize to, some conception of what the knee is like, or
some visualization of it, or even just an idea about its location. You'll want to practice reducing these concepts by recognizing the sensations that arise in relation to them and
allowing those sensations until you feel a sense of completion, and the tendencies arising out of your conceptions are
dropped.

When you relate to something, you will have concepts of
it. We all have prejudices, not only about race and gender but
also about knees and hearts, time and space. Recognize these
conceptions in yourself and reduce them. If you believe certain things about your event, you will act differently than if
you had no such ideas. If you conceive of your client as a man,
that he is lying down in front of you, that he is of a certain age
and stature, and that his particular problem is a difficult one,
you will carry these concepts into the relation, and they will

color the relation and define some of what you experience. We all have such tendencies, and some are so subtle that they might never be recognized in everyday affairs. But they color those affairs and affect every aspect of our lives. When they are present in the healing relationship they have significant consequences. Essentially, in healing or elsewhere, our tendencies and preconditions are the obstacles to transcendence.

It is like being in the cave, in the dark, unable to perceive fully. Even when we come out of the cave and have had some experience of an expanded consciousness, we still feel an urge to run back in, to suffer in the same ways, with the same old concepts, and to organize our perception of reality according to the old prejudices. But there is an escape from all this. You have subtle prejudices and presuppositions: that your client is lying there in front of you, that he is a certain distance away, that something is supposed to happen now, or that you are the instrument of that. Such suppositions are indeed subtle and you may have difficulty understanding them as prejudices.

Research this. Attempt to understand how these beliefs act to limit your possibilities, how they cause you to sense in a certain way and how those sensations are the sensations of resistance. It is as if the part of your consciousness that includes the concept is still in the dark and there is a block to the free flow of experience. The concept holds a tendency in the relation and this is a limitation. You become entrapped in the tendency and the tendency begins to direct the flow of your consciousness. So, to progress with this work, endeavor to recognize these tendencies and the concepts or presuppositions behind them. The only condition that we can allow in our system is that there can be no conditions.

Letting Go of Prejudice

An ironic example of this lies in the fact that we have used the sensitive space as a way to arrive at the Sacred Space, but if we feel that the sensitive space is a necessity for healing then it has also become a condition and a limiting belief. The sensitive process is an excellent tool and yet, if you are attached to it, if your concept is that it is necessary, then it is not very useful at all. It is the same with all such concepts. There is an understandable but unfounded fear of emptiness: the fear that without our concepts, definitions, or a point of view we would simply disappear. But we don't need to avoid the emptiness; we only have to drop our fear of it and our attachment to the forms that we are so familiar with. Emptiness is just the lack of presuppositions, and there is nothing unsafe in that. The state of no concepts is mercly a state of innocence. Without concepts you will continue to respond to whoever or whatever is occurring in your space; you just won't respond according to a preestablished model. Letting go of form is not a problem but attachment to form is. Your job now is to leave the forms behind and establish your healing presence by going into the transcendent state of formlessness.

⚔ REDUCE THE RESISTANCE

Tune in now and open your space. Touch your partner, and individualize to his or her leg. Working with the leg you will see that you might perceive a certain distance between you and the leg or that you might hold other preconceptions about the leg. Feel how it is that you experience these preconceptions, how they are expressed through your sensations, and recognize that these feelings are a resistance. Allow these sensations to happen as you would any other sensations. Notice, for example, how the distance between you and the leg feels and accept those sensations as resistance. Research how you feel the leg: the distance, the separation, and so on, and deal with it all as resistance.Work with this, noticing how there is an image of that separation being produced in your brain, a sense of it.Then release it. Reduce the resistance, reduce the image, and reduce the preconceptions that limit consciousness.

Continue to do this in all your practice sessions. Keep trying to recognize whatever stands in the way of your direct experience of the event. Deal with that as resistance, until the relation becomes pure and there is no distance at all, no difference between you and the experience. Learn to recognize some of your preconceptions and tendencies outside of practice, in everyday situations. Release them as you would if you were in a healing session.This will prove to be most liberating—one more place where your service as a healer will prove healing to you.

When you release all conditions in relation to your event, consciousness and experience can become one. Notice that when you introduce an intention, for example to balance the liver function, there will be conceptions of "liver" and of "balance."Acknowledge that resistance and reduce it without fighting it. Just reduce it. If you have the intention to heal, as we always do in Sat Nam Rasayan, recognize your preconceptions of healing and deal with them as well. If your intent is to reduce tenderness, or increase the effectiveness of the immune system, these intentions will also come with images attached. You will discover preconceptions in just about everything. In everyday consciousness some of these preconceptions are useful. Without them we would have to examine every bit of input to know what was important, what was dangerous, what was interesting, and so on.We would probably be crazy from the stress of that and completely unable to function. But in healing it is totally different. To establish a healing presence we need to have no prejudice whatsoever.

I recently treated a woman with breast cancer. Upon opening the space and individualizing to her tumor, I became aware of my tendency to locate it to a place in her body and mentally connect it to the lymph system. In relation to those preconceptions I recognized certain sensations across my upper chest, from shoulder to shoulder, that had a "sour" feeling associated with them. As I allowed these sensations I became more stable but other images, other concepts, continued to arise for a while. I saw a picture of a breast; I felt a blackness that I interpreted as disease. I felt myself as separate from these things, looking at them. After a time these images slowed down, and finally they stopped altogether. When they did I began to know the breast, know the tumor. This was peace; I could pause, rest, remain silent. There was nothing to understand, nothing to believe, and nothing to do. This was a place of intensity, a place of knowing something that never existed in just this way before and would never exist in this way again. I "knew" this event needed my intention that the heart chakra be opened and balanced. As I introduced that intention there was a feeling of fire. I felt as if I had turned into a flame of pure white heat. I could allow this intensity; it was not something that I resisted. It took some time, but slowly there was a sense of cooling, and then it was done.

CHAKRAS

A GOOD WAY to further your practice is to work with the chakras. You can begin to understand chakras one through five from the discussion on the elements. Each of the first five chakras corresponds to one of the elements. The first chakra, at the base of the spine in the region of the perineum, is associated with the earth element. The second chakra, at the region of the sex organs, is associated with water. The third chakra, at the navel and solar plexus, is where the fire element resides. The fourth chakra, at the heart, is the chakra of air. And the fifth chakra, at the throat, is the ether chakra.

The sixth chakra is also known as the third eye or the *ajna*, which means "to perceive." It is located at the center of the brow and is associated with the brain and pituitary gland. A well-developed ajna chakra manifests in intellectual and psychic ability, imagination, vivid dreaming, and perceptiveness. Unbalanced function here is associated with intellectual stagnation, mental disease, difficulty in focusing mental energy, headache, visual difficulties, and nightmares. One who operates from his or her sixth chakra is intuitive. This person might be a planner, a thinker, a visionary, in touch with the Divine. The sixth chakra is the center of light and imagery. This is a realm that can take us beyond the physical. With the power of this chakra we can enter the past or future, and can travel to the far corners of the universe. When operating out of the ajna chakra the mind can reach a state of pure awareness and deep intuition.

The seventh chakra is located at the top of the head and is the chakra of bliss, of oneness with God. This is also the center of thought. Thought is the first, primal, perceptible, but still immeasurable manifestation of the universal consciousness. We are made up of consciousness and are surrounded by consciousness. The seventh chakra is where we tap into this force, where we open to it, and feel its all-pervading presence. The activity of this chakra is meditation, the process through which consciousness knows itself. Meditation is also the way that the seventh chakra develops. When balanced and functioning well, this is the place of knowing and understanding on the highest levels. When it is out of balance one might be closed-minded, worried, depressed, or confused. In extreme malfunction of the seventh chakra one might experience insanity and psychosis.

My teacher, Yogi Bhajan, has also introduced the idea of an eighth chakra, not associated with the physical body at all but with the aura, the subtle energy field that surrounds the body. This is our projection and our protection, the sum of the energies of all the other chakras. A strong aura or eighth chakra is associated with health and success and is built through spiritual practice. When the aura is weak one may be quite vulnerable to outside negative forces and unable to protect oneself from disease. You probably know people who have very weak projections, who always look fragile, and you know others who, without ego or bravado, are a strong presence in any situation. These two types represent those with weak and those with strong auras.

I don't give this brief introduction to the chakras so that you might visualize them or have fixed ideas about them, as that would only encourage preconceptions in your work as a healer. In Sat Nam Rasayan it is not necessary to have a body of knowledge, whether it be about chakras or anatomy and physiology. You can work quite well without it. In fact, in the beginning this knowledge could easily lead you to the very preconceptions you have been trying to disavow. Nevertheless, later on it will help you to communicate with clients and other healers, and it will let you individualize more effectively, focusing your treatments where they are going to be the most useful. Knowledge of chakras can give greater accuracy to your intent. It is the same with a knowledge of psychological conditions or of anatomy, physiology, disease states, or any other information you may have about the body or mind. The more that you know about these, the more you will be able to communicate and the more you will be able to focus your treatment.

With more advanced knowledge, plus a great deal of practice with Sat Nam Rasayan, you will find that you can diagnose and suggest treatments and self-care other than the Sat Nam Rasayan treatments themselves. Essentially, knowledge will simply appear in your treatments. Unfortunately, your concepts, whatever you think or believe, are also likely to appear, and you will need to discriminate between knowledge and belief. It is very easy to relate to the sensations that come from your conceptions and to mistakenly believe that they are pure experience. This is one of the biggest challenges in learning to establish your healing presence and treat with Sat Nam Rasayan. Please be careful. Knowledge—of chakras, physiology, or your client's history—can lead you to confusion.

If you want to work with the chakras, you will need to research your preconceptions of them, just as you ought to understand other preconceptions. You will need to recognize these as your resistance to a direct relation to the chakras. Reduce these resistances, and then reduce them still more. It is perhaps easier to practice this with the chakras because they do not have an actual physical presence, as the heart or the brain does. Organs are very easy to imagine, but with chakras we can more easily acknowledge that our images are symbolic. An image of a chakra as a sphere with rays of colored light emanating from it might be easier to recognize as a preconception than would an image of the heart as a throbbing blood red organ. If you have already worked a lot with chakras you might have some attachment to your images or feelings about them. We carry a good deal of nonsense in our minds that we keep trying to apply to reality.

Research your preconceptions. In relation to the third chakra, for example, what do you believe? Perhaps you think, "subtle energy happening at the solar plexus," or "the source of personal power." Then those concepts are a source of resistance in your relation to the chakra. When you individualize to your client's third chakra, this will be a part of the resistance that you have to reduce.

To deal with this resistance, first become aware of the sensations that are resulting from your preconceptions. Become aware of the tendencies in your consciousness and then allow them to happen until you are stable. Individualize the chakra and renounce all your preconceptions of it. Recognize, for example, your sense of distance from the chakra and recognize all the information about the chakra that you might have carried into the relation. When you are no longer differentiated from the chakra you are working with, you will start to have the experience of the consciousness *in the chakra*, and this will allow the treatment to be completed. This is also when you may have an understanding of what else you can do, what other intents or movements you might introduce.

BEYOND THE
SENSITIVE SPACE

ONCE you have had the opportunity to experience the Sacred Space for yourself, by working directly with Guru Dev or one of the student-teachers of Sat Nam Rasayan, begin to practice going directly into the Sacred Space. Don't use the sensitive space at all. This will be a challenge, as you may have come to rely on the sensitive space. Now I am asking you to consider dropping the use of the sensitive space as your method. It is not that you are not to have sensations, for they will always be there, it is just that the sensitive space has perhaps become a pattern, and there can be no patterns. This is the Fifth Dogma: there are no dogmas. So try to be in the Sacred Space without this dogma of the sensitive space. You see, it may be difficult to reduce the differentiation between yourself and your event if you are trying to feel the other through your sensitive space.

This may be confusing to you. We said earlier that the only thing we know is our sensations. But what we are saying now is that you can directly experience the event, your client's third chakra, or her tumor. You can do that by experiencing the consciousness in the chakra itself or in the tumor itself. You do not experience it in you, if "you" is defined as an arbitrarily circumscribed region of sensations bounded by your skin. Rather, the event is experienced in consciousness. Your consciousness and the consciousness that is happening in the event are the same, and they are experienced in the same way. You will be working and will not know where you are in relation to the event. You won't quite know who is sitting up and who is lying down. You will ask your consciousness how the client is, and you will experience the client as the client experiences herself, or you will experience the heart chakra or the tumor as it experiences itself. So your consciousness of what is happening in the event is a sensitive experience, but it comes from the event's consciousness of itself. Put another way, by being in the Sacred Space you are not limited to consciousness of your own sensations but can, as you individualize, become conscious of the experience that your event is having. Your consciousness and the consciousness that is happening in your event are intimately intertwined, and you will experience them in the same way—sensitively, in the space of the relation.

Obviously, this is a radical departure from everyday awareness. This is a transcendent awareness, without the familiar boundaries. The sensitive process has brought you to the brink of this experience, but there is a mystery as to how the leap over that brink is to be made. I can suggest that you do not try to make the leap, as trying is not going to help. Effort is not required. It is more a matter of zero effort, plus intent, plus alert awareness, plus completely letting go, plus being linked to the lineage of Sat Nam Rasayan through the teacher. This is a state of nonduality, a state of emptiness, with no identification of self. The difficulty is that you may have become attached to the joys of the sensitive space and might not want to give it up just yet. You have filtered your experience through the sensitive process and now it can become a limitation, as if it were a requirement. But, beyond

Beyond the Sensitive Space

this limitation, there is the capacity for you to experience the consciousness in the event. So try to identify and release all of your concepts: that is necessary if you wish to transcend.

If you were treating a client for headache you might experience the distance between you and the client's head. You would say that the head is "there." This is an opportunity because in this you can recognize the concept of distance as a resistance, and you can reduce that resistance in the same way that you reduce any resistance. You recognize it and allow it until it is resolved. Then the head will appear without the condition of distance. Then you will notice the next resistance, perhaps that you consider the head to be congested. Consider that a resistance and release it also. Continue, moving from condition to condition. You will find that you don't really need to release every one of your conditions because after a few, the very tendency to have these conditions is broken. At that moment you will experience the head in the same way as you experience your own consciousness, without differentiation. It is not that you will be unable to tell the difference between your head and the client's head; it is more similar to how you might experience your own head and your foot at the same time. You know which is which but you can experience the consciousness in both of them.

The only way to be able to do this is to be stable. If your consciousness is moving, it won't happen. This is why it is important to have practiced with the sensitive process first, so that you can be stable. Even if you have practiced with the sensitive space for a long while, when you try to go to this new space that has no differentiation, you will need to go slowly. First, break the conditions or preconceptions of the sense of differentiation between you and the event. Then, begin to work at dropping the condition of the sensitive space. It is too much to try to do both at the same time.

157

As you do all this work you will notice that you continue to have feelings and sensations. But you will also notice that the feelings are not how you know what you know. They are there but the knowledge is yours simply because you are in the Sacred Space, because you exist without conditions. Before Sat Nam Rasayan, every experience you had was compared and contrasted to your conceptions. If an event affected you in a particular way, with particular sensations arising, then you interpreted that event as having a certain meaning. Next, in the beginning of your training as a healer, you recognized that every event was expressed in you in a sensitive way. Your reaction was probably some joy and pleasure at the richness of your experience, as you could feel everything in a new and more sensitive way. Now it is time to go on, beyond even that. It is time to become even more stable and then to reduce any differentiation by the method I have just described, the method of reducing the resistance due to preconceptions. If you go through this, you will find knowledge. You will escape from the limitations of your own sensations, you won't be hampered by your old points of reference, and you will heal because you will know the consciousness in the event and how to modify it.

The task now is just to keep practicing and dealing with resistance. Deal with the sensitive space as resistance, deal with your concepts as resistance, deal with your point of view and the sense of distance as resistance. Keep it up, releasing all concepts, until you are directly in relation with the event. In order to say that you have learned Sat Nam Rasayan you will need to be able to leave the sensitive space behind, to let it dissolve. The sensitive space is very pleasant, too pleasant perhaps, and it is hard to leave behind. Nevertheless it is a resistance and needs to be released.

HELPING WITH SERIOUS ILLNESS

WHEN working with serious illness, it is often best to work with the symptoms rather than with the overall disease. Reduce the symptoms and establish as much peace and balance as you can. Sat Nam Rasayan can be very good in a crisis, when things are quite chaotic. You can work on reducing inflammation or on relaxing anxiety and muscle tension, for example, and be very helpful.

HIV patients in particular need to be relaxed and need help with their symptoms. If the illness is advanced, this is especially true. With those who are recently infected, you can be more effective working to increase immune function. Later on, the work you do might be more about anxiety and emotional issues and about the side effects of the drugs they have taken. Treatments can be long (about three quarters of an hour) and frequent (every day at first, decreasing over time to about once a week). If a patient is terminal, with AIDS or another disease, you can work on him every day, up until the time of death. It is not a matter of prolonging the lives of these patients, although that may possibly be happening; it is more a matter of improving the life that there is, regardless of its length. Quality of life is more important than anything. If a patient has increased peacefulness and awareness, and less pain, then I think the treatments are successful.

If, beyond that, their life is also extended, that is good, but first treat the pain and release the other symptoms. First give people peace.

Sooner or later everyone dies, but that death will be then; it is not now. Now is when the patient must live. Many who are terminally ill don't live well because they know that they will die soon. These patients need help in coming into the present moment, in dealing with what is happening now. You can help them to do that with Sat Nam Rasayan.

Deal with the anxiety, deal with the symptoms, make the patient more aware, help her to face her denial, but don't try to give false hope. Find the balance of this in yourself. It is better to be innocent, to deal with the patient as you find him, not in terms of the name of his disease or of his prognosis. Go deeply into the patient and release whatever you can. Investigate the main symptoms and treat them; release the toxicity from the drugs, release the anxiety. Then you can go on to try to increase the immune function. It is also powerful with many HIV patients to introduce the intention of increasing self-esteem.

Another thing to do with HIV and other serious illness is to teach the client and his caregivers Sat Nam Rasayan. There are not enough healers, and we can't make enough of a difference. Critical patients need treatment a few times a week and there are too many people infected, too many with cancer, too many sick with all sorts of terrible diseases. The individual healer can only do a little, so we try to teach more and more people so that we can multiply ourselves and more can benefit. There is a certain minimum training that is needed for people to get results, but the information in this book is more than enough. Sat Nam Rasayan can be done in a very simple way and still have a worthwhile effect.

Helping with Serious Illness

A good rule in Sat Nam Rasayan is to deal with the obvious first. If a patient has a fever, try to reduce that first, before looking into the cause. This is not the way that one might want to practice medicine, but in Sat Nam Rasayan we work in this way. Reduce the fever, then the headache that is also there, then go into the underlying disease, then into the tendencies that produced the disease, then into the karma that produced the tendencies. This way, each time you work, you are providing relief. If a patient is depressed, reducing symptoms will reduce depression. When I was practicing dentistry many of my patients with chronic pain were depressed. They were also angry at physicians who wanted to treat the depression but not the pain. Their statement would always be something like, "Of course I'm depressed, who wouldn't be, with so much pain?" So reduce the symptoms and then treat the depression, if it is still there.

When a patient is dying, it is not going to be useful to try to stop that. It is much better to help the patient to die—to focus his or her consciousness. There is no use in lying to dying patients. They know that they need to prepare, so don't distract them from that work with thoughts about what they will do when they are better. There is no time for that, so do what is important in this moment. Help the patients resolve what is bothering them. Help them focus their consciousness, and resolve their anxiety, or whatever is not resolved in them. Your real value to these people will be if you can help produce awareness.

It is necessary for someone witnessing death in others to recognize his or her own fear. Each of us has some fear of death, and we must deal with the resistance that the sensations of fear produce. Recognize this in yourself and then you will be better able to talk with others about their fears. But if someone is depressed, don't add your own depression. Help her find her pain, recognize it, and allow the sensations of it. Explore with her what the pain is like, when in the past she has had similar feelings, and how she might be trying to avoid her feelings. Help her to just feel, without avoidance, and the pain will lessen.

In treating someone with anxiety, fear, or any other emotional state, individualize to that condition just as you might to any other condition. Individualize and be aware of your own resistance and discomfort and allow that to happen. Recognize the anxiety, or whatever you are working on, as your event and allow your sensations while holding yourself stable. Keep going deeper, allowing more sensations to happen. Research your own resistance to going deeper and allow that, with neither avoidance nor concentration.

You can also work on yourself with Sat Nam Rasayan. The only thing you need to be able to do is see yourself as your own event. If you have a pain in your leg and want to heal it, you will need to feel what you feel in relation to what you feel in your leg. Your leg pain becomes your event, just as if it were pain in your friend's leg. Recognize that the pain is there and is affecting you in a certain way. Feel how else you feel in relation to the pain in your leg. When you reduce the resistance to the feelings, the tendencies that have produced the pain will be reduced, and the pain will disappear. You can also do this with difficult emotional states in yourself. The key is to reduce your resistance—that will reduce the resistance in your event. By this point you should have found that reducing your resistance to sensations is relaxing to the client. It will also be relaxing to your own emotional pain or to the pain in your leg.

A FINAL WORD

BEYOND this I leave it to you to explore and research the effects of your treatments. Build up your own experience. Make no claims, but just offer your healing presence to others. Give them the opportunity to be in your presence as you enter the sensitive space or the Sacred Space on their behalf. Give yourself the opportunity to serve.

We exist in an unlimited space and in this space there is an unlimited energy, energy that is not at all the energy of the ego. This energy is without center, is always in flow, and is present whether it is observed or not. It is eternal and all-consuming, creative and healing. Remarkably, given its other characteristics, this energy's capacity to impose itself into the awareness of an individual is severely limited by ego. In the presence of ego this energy immediately appears stagnant, unable to flow, solidified, narrowed, and restricted. In effect, the puny ego eclipses the energy as the moon can eclipse the sun, not truly overwhelming it but hiding it from view. But like an eclipse, the effect is temporary and requires the continued presence of the ego. In the instant that the moon moves on, the sun reappears. In the moment that the ego is stilled, this healing energy reemerges.

Sat Nam Rasayan is the practice of stilling the ego. Then

consciousness can become aware of the reality of this underlying flow of energy. In the Sacred Space we are enabled to
have an extraordinarily direct relationship with what is happening, with being, with reality itself. This relationship is
based on egolessness. We have called this state the Sacred
Space, Sat Nam Rasayan, and unconditional love. We have
recognized it as the essence of the consciousness of healing.
And we have laid out a method, a simple path, that anyone
with devotion and dedication can follow to establish a healing presence. This is the path of the sensitive process.

Now it is up to you. As I have said over and over in these
pages, the descriptions and instructions I have given can only
point you in the right direction. To arrive at the destination,
to pierce the veil of unknowing and arrive suddenly at the remote target of transcendence, requires that you do the work
of the sensitive process. Practice every day. Become increas-
ingly comfortable with the process as you develop over a period of time. Try to begin a regular practice of Kundalini Yoga
as taught by Yogi Bhajan. This will go a long way in helping
you to be stable. Other forms of yoga and meditation will
help with your stability, but the Kundalini techniques are
especially effective. If it is at all possible, attend workshops
with Guru Dev Singh or one of the student instructors of Sat
Nam Rasayan. The Resources section that follows will give
you phone numbers to call for information about classes and
workshops.

There are other ways, of course, other paths to healing,
but this path that I have been privileged to describe is most
excellent and it is available to you here and now. Travel it in
service and joy.

Sat Nam.

RESOURCES

The following sources will be helpful to you as you establish yourself in a regular spiritual practice and continue your studies of Sat Nam Rasayan.

For information about healing sessions, classes, workshops, and retreats with Guru Dev Singh or student instructors under his direction, call 213-655-2088 (Los Angeles) or 396-904-1478 (Rome).

For the name of a Kundalini Yoga teacher in your area (worldwide) call The International Kundalini Yoga Teachers Association at 505-753-0423.

For a free catalog of excellent products related to yoga, meditation, and healing, including a large selection of Kundalini Yoga and Meditation books and instruction manuals, call Ancient Healing Ways at 800-359-2940.

To order additional copies of this book or Subagh Khalsa's other books (*Meditation for Absolutely Everyone* and *The Success of the Soul: A Guide to Peace, Purpose, and Prosperity*), both of which are packaged along with audiotapes that help guide your meditation practice, please call the publisher, Tuttle Publishing, at 800-526-2778.

For information about workshops, classes, retreats, seminars, or private sessions with the author, please contact him at 716-473-0199 or through either the publisher or the International Kundalini Yoga Teachers Association.